MW01600856

Volume 1

LOVERS *of* HOLINESS PUBLICATIONS

FAITH PAPERS

A Treatise On Experimental Aspects of Faith

Samuel Ashton (S. A.) Keen

Of The Cincinnati Conference
Methodist Episcopal Church Residence
Delaware, O.

FAITH PAPERS

A Treatise On Experimental Aspects of Faith

Samuel Ashton (S. A.) Keen

LOVERS

HOLINESS

PUBLICATIONS

Printed By
KDP – An Amazon.com Company USA
Imprint: Independently Published
ISBN: 9798856732770

Table of Contents

The Way To Faith

The Fulness of Faith

Introduction

An acquaintance with the nature of evangelical faith and the mode of its exercise is the most important of all knowledge. The deepest familiarity with politics and history, the profoundest intimacy with ethics and, philosophy, the greatest proficiency in the arts and sciences, and the most brilliant exploits in statesmanship and military achievements, will fail in happifying and saving the soul, and must go out in darkness without a sin-conquering faith. To fail at the mercy-Seat, where faith alone can succeed, is to fall everywhere and forever.

Every careful reader of the Scriptures has not failed to notice that much greater efficiency than appears in the Churches is graciously tendered to the saints. And under this light the general Christian heart yearns, by the promptings of the Holy Spirit, to realize in experience and work the Savior's statement, "He that believeth on me, the works that I do shall he do also; and greater works than these shall he do." All earnest Christians long for this gift, but, through spiritual blindness, many are searching for it where it can never be found. It is not to be found in travel amidst classic ruins, nor in the learning furnished by the schools of philosophy, nor the knowledge obtained in the seminaries of theology, nor yet in the wisdom of methods and plans. Nothing succeeds here but that meek, lowly, and humble faith discussed in these pages, and which unites its subjects to the risen, glorified, and almighty Christ. Hence any effort that promises success in spreading the knowledge of this all-important grace ought to have the encouragement and support of the universal Church.

Great numbers who read the " FAITH PAPERS," as they appeared in the different issues of the now extinct Beulah Land, testified to their great worth and the benefit which they received from them, and congratulated the author upon his happy method of presenting and elucidating the subject of faith. Now that these "papers" are to be given to the Church in a more durable form, and with conditions for much wider distribution, it is gratifying to know that they must enter upon a much larger mission of usefulness.

The subject is so thoroughly analyzed, the points are so well taken, the different phases of the grace so well illustrated, and all brought into such narrow compass, that the mass of Christian readers can command the work, can understand the subject, and must be greatly edified and helped in their spiritual life by the perusal of the book. The author, and the friends of wholesome religious literature, may feel assured that He who guided in writing the "papers," has His hands also upon their publication and circulation, and will glorify Himself by this contribution to the means of Christian enlightenment.

Sheridan Baker Coshocton, Ohio

Preface of S. A. Keen

These "Faith Papers" are designed to present experimental aspects of faith. Hence, they are written in the terms of experience rather than those of doctrine. They have, however, as the author believes, a sound Scriptural and doctrinal basis. Each of these Papers is adapted to meet a definite soul-want. They are spiritual specifics for the cure of some form of unbelief. The first five treat of Saving Faith, and the last five of Special Faith. The thought of these Papers was evolved by the author when driven to special prayer and searching of the Word of God in the midst of a continuous revival work, as a presiding elder in the Ohio Conference. May they scintillate the holy glow of the hallowed flame whence they sprang! These Papers first appeared in a now extinct periodical, "The Beulah Land." Subsequently, the first five were published in tract form. The circulation of these brought so many testimonials of their helpfulness to souls, together with so many requests from able ministers and eminent Christian workers that they be given permanent form, and having for five years waited to carefully review and apply the faith-principles herein taught in pastoral evangelistic work, the author now commits them in this volume to the Church, devoutly praying that they may have the sanction of the Holy Spirit as they go forth to the world.

S. A. Keen
Roberts Park, Indianapolis, Ind., June 1, 1888

Preface of Lovers of Holiness Convention

In June of 1888 the Free Christian Baptist Association of Atlantic, Canada met for what they called "The Deliverance Conference." They brought to the floor for debate five ordained elders who had experienced a second, definite work of grace following their conversion, where they received the blessing of a pure heart. These five brethren were testifying to and preaching the grace of entire sanctification. History proves, and 1888 was no exception, the preaching of entire sanctification, and holiness of heart and life, produces conviction and controversy. These five brethren were "disfellowshipped." As a result, these men called for a gathering for "the lovers of holiness" in Woodstock, New Brunswick, Canada on November 1, 1888, and seventy-five people gathered. The effects of that meeting were felt for a couple of generations.

In 2020. a couple of brethren began to pray and discuss the need for a convention that would center around the Bible doctrine of entire sanctification and separation from the world. The congregation of Trinity Bible Holiness Church near Pleasantville (Alum Bank), PA agreed to host the first convention in 2021 and the convention continues to meet annually near Bedford, PA. The purpose of this gathering is to provide an atmosphere for preaching, worship, and fellowship for the lovers of old fashioned, second blessing holiness. May God grant us strength of purpose to be of the same spiritual vigor as those brethren in the first lovers of holiness gathering in 1888.

Chapter 1: The Way To Faith

Romans xi, I: "I beseech you therefore, brethren, by the mercies of God, that ye present your bodies a living sacrifice, holy, acceptable unto God, which is your reasonable service."

There are states of heart which render faith impossible. An impenitent heart, a willful heart, or an unconsecrated heart is incapable of believing unto salvation. To say to a soul in the heyday of sin; or to an unawakened heart, or to an enlightened child of God who refuses to give himself wholly to the Lord, "Believe, and thou shalt be saved," is to expect him to do what he cannot do. His state of heart is obstructive to faith. No man can believe unto salvation when he will, irrespective of his condition of heart. There are essential antecedents to the exercise of faith. There are states of heart which lead to faith. The attainment of these is the way to faith. There are two steps to faith for a soul under gospel illumination.

The first is conviction. Only the soul that is feelingly conscious of its unsaved condition, its spiritual destitution, and its utter moral helplessness is capable of laying hold of the promises of God so as to rest in them alone for salvation. Inwrought conviction makes the soul reach out beyond itself for help and makes it willing to accept the Divine Word as its sure support against despair. Such conviction, either for the guilt of sin or the presence of inbred sin in the soul, as brings a sense of extreme need of salvation, is the heart-pang by which faith is begotten. When such a crisis of conviction is reached, faith becomes such a necessity to the soul that it must believe. In the distress of such spiritual emergency, it instinctively cries out: "Lord, I believe; help thou mine unbelief." It was in the throes of heart-rending conviction that the jailer at Philippi believed and was saved. Never did Dr. Adam Clarke believe unto full salvation until his soul became so agonizingly conscious of inbred sin, and so painfully desirous for deliverance from it, as that he felt he must believe and be saved or superadd to his sin of heart the condemnation and darkness of unbelief. This first step in the way to faith is a short one; it may be quickly taken. Do you say: "I am waiting for conviction?" Then, it will never come; it never comes to those who are waiting for it. It only comes to those who want it, who invite it, who seek it. Anyone who accepts God's Word as the voice of the Holy Spirit speaking to him, if he is either an unforgiven sinner or an unsanctified believer, can in a little while be filled with so much conviction as will make him long for salvation more than they who watch for the morning. Let the impenitent soul come face to face with a few of God's commands and appeals, such as "Turn ye, why will ye die?" "Be ye also ready," "The wages of sin is death," "He that believeth not shall be damned," and take them to heart as his, and he will very soon have such a sense of lostness as will make him cry out, I must, I will believe. Let a believer who is not fully saved think upon the words of the Lord, "Be ye holy, for I am holy," "Without holiness no man shall see the Lord," "Wash you, make you clean," and there will come to his heart such a sense of unlikeness to God and unfitness for heaven as will make him cry out, "O wretched man that I am, who shall deliver me from this body of death?" and will bring him where faith must lend its victorious power. We challenge any truly converted person who is walking in the light of the witness of the Holy Spirit to his acceptance with God, but has not the witness of heart-purity, and is skeptical in respect to the existence of inbred sin in the soul and the need of full salvation, to consent to such a divine inspection as David subjected himself to when he laid bare his heart unto the eyes of him with whom we have to do, and said: "Search me, O God, and know my heart; try me and know my thoughts, and see if there be in me any wicked way." He will not have waited long in that powerful light until he will begin to plead, "Create in me a clean heart, O God," and will be ready to receive entire sanctification by faith.

A few years since I had in one of my Churches a class-leader. He was an excellent man; but in some way he had become pronounced in his skepticism respecting, and his opposition to, the experience of entire sanctification. He thought the doctrine of sin in believers a mere fancy. He was doubtless honest in all his misconceptions and unbelief. It was all the more difficult to bring him to a right way of thinking, for he was useful and consistent in his life. I yearned to see him brought into the fullness of God's love. We never argued or contended together on the subject. We lived and labored together in love. About a year and a half after I became his pastor, we were having an evening meeting at which were present over two hundred of my members. The theme turned on heart-searching. After some remarks to the effect that we are incapable to search our own hearts, that God alone can search the heart and bring to the light of our consciousness what of evil or good may be hidden from our most careful introspection, I proposed that we all bow before God and silently wait for such revelation respecting our hearts as he might give while we should breathe into his ear the prayer: "Search me, O God." Every person in the congregation bowed, this beloved leader with the rest. No one led in prayer; each went to God for himself. In a few minutes sobs began to rise, first from one pew, then from another. The whole lecture-room became a Bochim, a valley of weeping. Having remained about ten minutes upon our knees, we arose. I said: " If anyone has discovered anything in your heart that has surprised you and that is painful to yourself, you may speak of it." Instantly this class-leader arose and exclaimed, "O, my heart, my heart I never knew that all this was in my heart pray for me," and fell upon his knees in the pew where he was standing. A season of prayer was held at once. A few days after, he found perfect cleansing from the sin which he had seen in his heart. Within six months after, on his dying bed, he constantly repeated,

"The cleansing stream, I see, I see! I plunge, and O, it cleanseth me."

He was not too swift in seeking a consciousness of indwelling sin and inward cleansing from it. They who would have a conscious sense of the guilt or the defilement of sin, without which they cannot believe unto Salvation, can soon attain it. The preaching, the Christian testimony, and godly admonitions which bring the most immediate and powerful conviction for outward and inward sin, will bring forth the most immediate fruit of faith.

The second step in the way to faith is consecration. To the awakened sinner this means self-surrender to God. He chooses his service, bows to his yoke, and cries: "I am thine; take me as I am." When this is accomplished, believing ground is reached where the soul easily and almost imperceptibly believes and is saved; though sometimes there is a struggle to believe after the surrender is complete, because Satan makes a powerful stand at this point against the soul, because one more step is to bring it out of his captivity. But the soul has come to the position that commands faith, and here it can rout the adversary by a desperate act of faith in saying: "I can, I will, I do believe."

To the believer that is seeking heart-purity this consecration means complete self-dedication to God. Without this, faith for cleansing is impossible. To attempt to believe unto full Salvation until all is put upon the altar of God, is useless effort and wasted time. When I was seeking a clean heart, the moment I got the consent of my heart to say, "I am thine, wholly thine for evermore," believing that the blood cleansed and that the altar sanctified, followed immediately and naturally. And I have never found any difficulty as I have walked in the way of holiness in believing, when I have been conscious of being wholly the Lord's.

We are so slow to take the final step of consecration. We hesitate and shrink from letting all go on to the altar which sanctifies the gift. Consecration is the offering of ourselves up to God according to his word. It need not take long -- it should not. Satan may say, "God requires more than you can give or do, your children, your property, your life;" reply: "God only requires what is best. He only demands a reasonable service."

The adversary will argue: "It is hard to give all to God." Joyfully rejoin: "His commandments are not grievous, and in keeping of them there is great delight." O soul, convinced of the need of heart cleansing, remember, if it be hard to the natural heart to give all to God, that it will prove harder yet to not make the consecration.

Said a sister to me, as her pastor: "I ought to wholly consecrate myself to God, but I can't." I replied: "Don't say you can't, but you won't." "Yes," she replied, "that is it; but I mean it is so hard." "True," said I; "but it is harder not to do it. Do it, and God will dwell in your heart, bless your home, and lead your children to salvation; but do it not, darkness will come to your soul, your children will grow up irreligious, and, possibly, you yourself will lie down and die without the hope of heaven." She refused to make the consecration, and my words proved prophetic. All the apprehended evils suggested came, and more; and suddenly one day she dropped out our life. O, how much harder it proved to her, as it will to any soul, not to consecrate itself to God, than to give all to him. Who then!

Dear reader, do you long to know the faith that brings full salvation. At once present yourself a living sacrifice to God, under the conscious need you feel to be cleansed from all sin, and you may at once believe unto righteousness. Do the eyes of any one fall upon these words, whose heart is sore with the unrest, the ache, the fearfulness of conviction for sin, and you are offering yourself up to God in complete consecration? You need wait no longer, only believe, resolutely trust the immutable word of the Lord, and your heart shall joyously shout:

"Hallelujah! 'tis done, I believe on the Son; I am saved by the blood of the crucified One."

Chapter 2: What To Believe

Romans x, 8: "The word is nigh thee, even in thy mouth and in thy heart: that is, the word of faith which we preach."

The thing to be believed, in seeking salvation, either in pardon or entire sanctification, is the WORD OF GOD, especially as embodied in the exceeding great and precious promises of the Bible. For this reason, the apostle Paul calls it (Rom. x, 8) the word of faith; that is, the word to be believed, and which, when believed, brings salvation. Often earnest seekers of salvation are exhorted to believe, to trust; just what they are most anxious to do, but they do not know what to believe. Hence their efforts to believe are like beating the air; they do not bring salvation. What all seekers need to have made known to them is, that the thing they are to believe is the WORD OF GOD. It is the only sufficient ground of faith; it is the "word of faith" whosoever believes it shall be saved.

When a boy thirteen years of age, I became deeply convicted of sin, and earnestly anxious to be saved. I went to an altar of prayer in the midst of a glorious revival of religion in my native town. There for three nights I sought the Lord in the pardon of my sins, All who spoke to me told me to believe, and nothing was I more anxious to do than to believe; yet no one told me what to believe. I presume they thought I knew; but I did not. Finally, on the third night of my struggle, an old saint of God came to me, and laying his patriarchal hands upon my head, as I bowed there bewildered and almost disheartened, he said: "Son, Jesus says if you come to him, he will receive you and save you; believe his word, and you shall be saved." I did it instantly, -- and as instantly the peace

of pardon and the joy of salvation filled my soul. Just so soon as I knew what to believe, I did it quickly, and was saved.

Praise the Lord, for the word of faith, which, when believed, brings salvation!

A few years since, a college friend, a graduate of the Ohio Wesleyan University, was bowing with many others as a seeker of full salvation. His conviction of inbred sin was pungent, and his struggle intense for deliverance from it. As I knelt by him to encourage and instruct him, he said: "O, give me a promise, give me a promise!" He seemed to know that he must believe God's Word in order to be saved fully, but Satan was just then so darkening his mind that his memory could not recall any one of its many precious promises, although he was well versed in the Scriptures, and was a superior Bible-class teacher. I repeated in his ear, as he was begging for a promise, this: "Wherefore he is able also to save them to the uttermost that come unto God by him." (Heb. vii, 25.) The words were scarcely off my lips before he exclaimed: "That is what I wanted; I believe it; praise the Lord, O my soul, I am fully saved." Ever since he has known the joy of a full salvation. This "word of faith" is sufficient. It is the word of the Lord, more immutable than the stars in their celestial order, or the eternal hills in their grand repose. "Heaven and earth shall pass away, but my words shall not pass away." This word is indorsed to us in the name of Jesus, written in his own blood. "All the promises of God in him are yea, and in him are amen!" This word is the very voice of the Holy Spirt speaking to our hearts. Whosoever believes it shall not be confounded.

"How firm a foundation, ye saints of the Lord, Is laid for your faith in his excellent word."

This "word of faith " is available. It is nigh thee," says the apostle, " even in thy mouth and in thy heart." It is the truth our minds have accepted, and our lips have professed, but which we have been slow to believe as the very word of God.

There is not a gospel-enlightened soul, either sinner or believer, but knows and has in his heart the word of truth, which is able to make him wise unto salvation. The word to be believed has been put in our mouths and lodged in our hearts by the instructions of home, or the teachings of the Sabbath-school, or the preaching of a living ministry. It is at hand. No new revelation, or interpretation, or further light of the Holy Spirit is essential to faith. The word is "nigh" us, even within us. Whosoever will believe shall be saved. This "word of faith" if effectual believed, it is found to be spirit and life. As chemical action immediately ensues when the proper fluids come in contact with the proper metals in the electrical jar, producing the ethereal fiery current, so the moment the soul believes the word of faith, spiritual action ensues; life, light, warmth, rest, satisfaction, instantly possess the heart. The full virtue of the word of faith passes at once into the soul when touched by its faith. The word when believed is immediately the power of God unto salvation to the soul.

If the word believed be, "He is just and faithful to forgive us our sins," the peace of pardon is at once realized. If it be, "Having these promises, let us cleanse ourselves from all filthiness of the flesh and spirit, perfecting holiness in the fear of the Lord," trusted, immediately, "Refining fire goes through the heart, Illuminates the soul; Scatters its life through every part, And sanctifies the whole."

Or should the word accepted in faith be, "Receive ye the Holy Ghost," the Pentecostal power suddenly fills the soul.

When, therefore, we believe the word of faith, simultaneously therewith is effectuated in us all the salvation, power, and blessedness proffered to us in the exceeding great and precious promises of God. For when received, not as the word of men, but as it is in truth, the word of God, it effectually worketh in them that believe. (See I Thess. ii, 13.) This has been verified times without number by God's children. Our peace is in believing; according to our faith it is done unto us; to them that believe, he is precious as a justifier, or sanctifier, or anointer, with power.

Mrs. Phoebe Palmer was wont to say: "The Holy Spirit speaks to my heart by the WORD, and when I believe it, I at once experimentally apprehend, as Jesus has said, that his words are spirit and life." Life effectual is the Word in any soul when believed by it.

Faith the mighty promise sees, and looks to that alone; Laughs at impossibilities, And cries: 'Hallelujah,' 'tis done!'"

A sufferer who was rapidly declining under the progress of a painful disease and had been earnestly seeking for the white robes of entire cleansing from sin in her heart, in which to meet the king in his beauty without abashment, said to me, as I entered her sick-room one morning: "Last night the Holy Spirit threw out to me a line of promise. I seized it, and I am now gloriously saved." Her abundant entrance into life eternal, a few weeks later, proved that her confidence in "the word of faith " was not misplaced, but brought the true end of faith, even the salvation of her soul. So, it is ever; just when the trembling sinner puts faith in some sweet promise of God's Word, he finds it,

"A sure support against despair." The moment the child of God, seeking full redemption in the blood of the Lamb, begins to sing,

"In the promises I trust," in the same breath will continue:

"Now I feel the blood applied;" "Jesus saves, he saves me now."

Dear reader, having come to the fountain of cleansing by a complete dedication of your soul and life to God, the way into its crimson flood is the way of faith; and the way of faith is to believe the Word of God; that is, accept it as true to yourself. The Holy Spirit now declares, "The blood of Jesus Christ cleanseth from all sin," and promises that according to your faith it shall be unto you. Dear soul, at once respond,

"Lord, I believe thy every word, Thy every promise true,"

and you shall know the joy of entire sanctification by faith alone. As you lay down this paper, may you at once enter the "way of faith," which is believing God's word.

Chapter 3: How To Believe

"All things are possible to him that believeth."

The faith which saves the soul is believing what God says and believing it because he says it. "Abraham believed God, and it was counted to him for righteousness." When God told him he was going to give him a son, Abraham, without any outward proof and "against hope," chose to believe God because he had said it, and according to his faith it was done unto him. God's word is his testimony concerning the divine purpose to save the soul that believeth in Jesus. "If we receive the witness of men (which we do), the witness of God is greater; for this is the witness of God which he hath testified of his Son. He that believeth on the Son of God hath the witness in himself; he that believeth not God hath made him a liar, because he believeth not the record that God gave of his Son." You say: "I know what is to be believed; that the infallible word of God is the sole ground of faith." But you ask: "Can I trust the word of the Lord?"

Does not the inquiry sound sacrilegious? and does not the echo of it almost startle you? Why can't a human heart trust the word of the Lord, if it will? God certainly does not enjoin as a sole condition of salvation a thing which it is impossible for us to perform. There is only one state of heart in which it is impossible for it to believe the word of God, and that is when it is unwilling to submit to God. The soul that gives itself up to God can believe his word, if it chooses to do so. But you say: "I have thought that saving faith is the gift of God." Then, you have thought wrong; for such is not the teaching of the Bible. It does say that "Ye are saved by grace through faith, and that not of yourselves; it is the gift of

God." But this teaches that the whole scheme of redemption -- that of salvation by faith -- is by the gracious favor of God, and not that the faith by which salvation is secured is the gift of God. Saving faith is not the gift of God in any proper sense.

The ability to believe, the power to trust God, belongs to every man, through the involuntary help of the Holy Spirit, vouchsafed by the atonement. But the exercise of this gracious capability devolves upon us. We have the power to believe, and have presented us the word of God, which is to be believed; and when we choose to believe that word, that is faith.

Saving faith is not a gracious state of the heart wrought by some sovereign power of the Holy Spirit; nor is saving faith a kind of an entity, a tangible something God bestows upon the heart, and then, in view of its presence in the soul, sends salvation. To expect God to give us faith in this sense is a forlorn hope, though we may pray for it; for faith is our own act. No one, not even God, can perform it for us. It is not a thing that can be given us; it is a thing to be done by us.

A few years since, during the progress of a revival in one of my churches, there was a man who had for twenty years been a regular attendant upon the services of a certain Christian Church; he was exemplary in his morality, had a warm feeling for God's people, and was a great Bible student. All during these years he had wanted to be saved, but having gotten the wrong notion that the faith which saves is the gift of God, he had been waiting for God to give him faith so that he could be saved. He was sitting one evening in my church while an interesting service was going on. I had occasion to remark, during its progress: "Jesus says, 'Trust me, I will save you;' and you say, 'I can trust thee, precious Savior; thou hast died for me.' That single remark led him to see that he had been waiting for faith to be given him, while Jesus had been waiting all these years for him to put faith in Him. I knew nothing of what was then transpiring in his mind until the service was through. After which he came up to me, his face bright, and taking my hand, he said: "Jesus has saved me!" I said: "When?" "O, just a few minutes ago. I have been wanting to be saved for twenty years, but have been waiting for God to give me faith; and when you said, 'Jesus says, "Trust me, and I will save you,"' I saw that for twenty years I had been waiting for God to put faith into me, when he had been waiting all these years for me to put faith in his word." He was very happy. It was the day of salvation to him.

It is a cheat of Satan to keep souls seeking salvation, either in conversion or entire sanctification, from the blessing they desire, by persuading them that they can't believe, and that God must give them faith before they can believe.

The soul can believe God. He has not fixed an unreasonable and impossible condition of salvation when he says: "Believe, and thou shalt be saved." He only requires what we can perform.

Faith being the exercise of the power we possess to believe God's word; it is a voluntary act. The soul must recognize that it can believe; must choose to believe must say, "I will believe;" and persistently reckon pardon or purity its own on God's word, in the face of every temptation to doubt, arising from any source whatever. In every struggle for salvation the soul will believe something, it will either believe the word of the Lord as whispered to it by the Holy Spirit, or it will believe the word of Satan whispered by his tempting voice. At every stage in seeking the Lord there is either defeat in believing Satan, or victory in believing Jesus. Faith is believing God. Doubt is believing Satan. We can resist a temptation to doubt, just as we can a temptation to envy, revenge, or uncharitableness. When the tempter says to the child of God who has been unjustly treated, "Seek revenge,"

"Be unforgiving," "Demand redress," let him say: "Get behind me, Satan, thou art an offense unto me; I will not indulge in envy or ill-will; I will not cherish bitterness." Thus, resisting the devil, through the Holy Spirit helping him, Satan will flee from him, and he is kept from falling into sin and marring his communion with God. So when Satan comes to the heart seeking salvation, and tempts it to doubt, saying, "You can't be saved; you are too bad, or have waited too long, or you can't keep salvation if you find it;" the soul thus buffeted by Satan must resist these insinuations of the adversary by clinging to the word of the Lord, which is able to save all them that believe it; and Satan will depart, leaving the soul in a sweet repose of trust and the consciousness of a precious salvation.

One evening, years since, I was called to visit a woman, well on in years, who was thought to be rapidly sinking under a very painful disease. She had been a stranger to me. On entering her room and taking her by the hand, I said: "How are you?" "O," she said, "I am suffering so; every nerve seems to be on fire, and I am not saved! O, I am so miserable!" The lines of suffering and despair blended together in her face. I said, "Are you asking the Lord to help you?" "O yes," she replied, "but Jesus doesn't help me. Sometimes it seems as though I am going to be saved, and it begins to get a little light; then something says, 'Jesus won't save you', and then it gets so dark." I said: "Mother, do you know when you begin to feel that Jesus is going to save you that it is because you begin to believe the words of Jesus which say, 'If you trust me I will save you;' then Satan begins to say, 'Jesus won't save you,' and you begin to believe Satan, and it gets so dark with you? Now, mother, when Satan says this, you say, 'Jesus will save me, for he says so, and I will believe him;' and reject the words of Satan. Doing this, the clouds will lift from your soul, and you will be saved." She was silent for a moment or two, and then calling to her daughter, who was in an adjoining room, she said: "Come here, daughter." Her daughter, half frightened, thinking she might be worse, hurried to her bedside. She exclaimed: "O, daughter! I am saved! All my darkness is gone, and my pains are gone; I am so happy! I just quit believing Satan, and O, Jesus has come to me!" Her joy was unspeakable. Her pains returned, but not her fears.

Within five minutes she came into a sweet, abiding faith by resisting the temptations of the adversary to doubt the word of the Lord. So, when Satan contradicts your seeking heart, saying, "You can't believe," "Jesus won't save you," resent this falsehood and say:

"I can, I will, I do believe that Jesus saves me now."

Are you a seeker of pardon? Take some promise of God's Word; make up your mind to believe it; say to yourself, what God says is true, whether you feel it to be so or not. God says: "If we confess our sins, he is faithful and just to forgive us our sins." You say, in the response of faith: "Lord, I choose to believe this; I will believe this; I do believe I am saved." And when Satan says, as he is most likely to do, "How do you know you are saved? do you feel it?" answer boldly: "No, I do not feel it at all, but it is so, for God says so; and I would rather trust his Word than my own feelings, however joyous." Resting thus unwaveringly on God's Word, though tempted by the adversary that your faith is not real, you will not wait long before the peace of pardon and the witness of acceptance will be given you.

Are you a child of God seeking full salvation?' Seize upon some declaration of God's Word, such as "The blood of Jesus Christ, his Son, cleanseth from all sin;" apply it to your own heart; confess to yourself, to Satan, and to God, that it is true to you, even you, because the Lord hath spoken it; refuse to listen to the lying voice of Satan that it is not so. Let no inward feeling or outward sign dissuade you from your voluntary choice to count God's Word true to yourself. And according to such a faith it shall be done unto you. What every seeking soul needs most to know is that it can believe unto salvation if it will; and that choosing to count God's Word as true in the face of every temptation to distrust it, is faith. Have you given all to Christ? Are you now longing to be fully saved? Are you persuaded that

"'Tis the promise of God Full salvation to give Unto him who on Jesus, His Son, will believe?"

You may at once begin to sing,

"I can, I will, I do believe that Jesus saves me now."

Should we lose every other line from the volumes of sacred song now existent, and this latter couplet remain, we could sing the world to pardon and the Church to purity. It contains the rationale and expresses the progress of faith from its beginning to its consummation. About a year since there was a lady who had been seeking the Lord for many months, but not finding the light, warmth, and rest of conscious salvation, had become so much discouraged that she had no heart to come forward longer to the altar of prayer. One evening she was sitting in her pew, dark and sad in her heart. An interesting consecration service was going on, in the midst of which was sung the chorus,

"I can, I will, I do believe That Jesus saves me now.

It had been repeated several times in connection with stanzas of that grand old salvation hymn: "Alas! and did my Savior bleed."

As the melody of its simple music reiterated it in her ears and heart, it came to her in power, and she began to say to herself: Why, yes, I can; why shouldn't I believe the Lord? I will; yes, I may, if I will. I do; yes, I do believe that Jesus saves me now." It was done. She was saved. Her soul was exulting in the Lord.

The method of faith is for the soul to recognize that it can believe God's word, then choose to believe it, which always carries it over to the consciousness: "I do believe." Believing is our part, and is antecedent; saving is God's part, and is consequent. All the blessed effects of faith, pardon, adoption, entire sanctification, are the Lord's doings, and are marvelous in our eyes; and they are all possible to him that believeth on the Son of God. Dear reader, as you lay down this paper, say: "Lord, I believe."

Glory to the Lamb!
"Thou dost this moment save, With full salvation bless."

Chapter 4: Its Elements

I John v, 10: "He that believeth on the Son of God hath the witness in himself."

The witness which the soul may have assuring it of salvation is twofold: 1st. The witness of faith; 2d. The witness of the Holy Spirit. By the mouth of these two witnesses, every soul is to be established in saving grace. The witness of faith is antecedent, the witness of the Holy Spirit subsequent. These two witnesses are concurrent. They bear testimony to salvation. The witness of faith is the conscious reception of salvation; the witness of the Holy Spirit is the conscious realization of salvation.

A gentleman fell heir very unexpectedly to an immense fortune. He could hardly believe that so much wealth had been bequeathed him. The legal papers were presented him, and on their testimony he accepted, received the bequest as his own, but could not realize that he was rich -- made so in a moment. When, however, he began to handle the moneys, and count the stocks, and control the lands into the possession of which he had come, then came to him the realization that he was rich, that he was a millionaire. The order of his experience was, first, the witness of faith; that is, the conscious reception of all this wealth on the testimony of the legal evidence. Then followed the conscious realization that he was, indeed, munificently endowed. So when the soul believes the exceeding great and precious promises of God's Word-that is, consciously accepts the heavenly treasure of salvation -- it has the witness of faith; it knows that it does receive salvation. But when the preciousness of this pearl of great price, the joy of the possession of this found treasure, the sweetness of saving power received, is consciously realized, it has the witness of the Holy Spirit.

The witness of faith is the John the Baptist which heralds and introduces the mightier witness of the Holy Spirit which cometh after it. The elements of the witness of faith are:

I. The soul's conscious acceptance of God's Word as true to itself; that is, the soul, irrespective of any outward sign or inward feeling, without any inner light or warmth, or witness previously given, accepts salvation on God's Word alone; it counts true to itself the promise, that whosoever believeth on the Son shall be saved. It does not ask that the infallible Word of the Lord, which shall endure, though heaven and earth pass away, shall be corroborated by any collateral surety. It accepts the Word as so sure and effective, as that all confirmation of its verity is not only unnecessary, but would be sacrilegious, if desired.

There is a beautiful incident in the life of Ahaz, king of Judah, which illustrates how faith accepts the Word of the Lord as true and disdains any collateral security. The kings of Syria and Israel had entered into a formidable alliance against Ahaz, and moved their combined forces against his capital, Jerusalem. When this was told Ahaz and his people, there was great consternation in the palace and the capital. "The heart of Ahaz and the heart of his people was moved as the trees of the wood are moved with the wind." In the midst of this crisis the prophet Isaiah was sent by the Lord to say to Ahaz: "Take heed and be quiet; fear not, neither be faint hearted, because Syria and Ephraim have taken evil counsel against thee. It shall not stand; neither shall it come to pass. If ye will not believe, ye shall not be established." At that moment the old king set his heart to believe the promise of the Lord which had just been given him, and accepted it as true to him and his capital.

Then the Lord spake to Ahaz and said to him: "Ask again; ask it either in the depths, or in the heights above." It was as though God had said to him, I will give you additional assurance, if you desire it. This was really a test of his faith; for faith is not made perfect, if the heart seeks something more than the Word of the Lord to command its confidence. The genuineness of Ahaz's faith then asserted itself, and he said in holy confidence: "I will not ask" (a sign); I ask no collateral security to God's Word; no sweeping whirlwind or crashing earthquake or descending fire do I ask; it is the Word of the Lord, and it shall come to pass.

But how many seeking hearts, to whom God has given his Word, that according to their faith it shall be done unto them, ask a sign, a warmth, a light, a witness, or some other inward phenomenon, before they are ready to accept the Word of the Lord as true; but none is ever given. Whoever consciously accepts the Word of the Lord as true to himself, will have the witness of faith in himself to his salvation.

A professor in a university on the Pacific Coast had been for ten years a seeker of full salvation but did not come into its enjoyment. One day an aged minister, traveling in the interest of the American Bible Society, was stopping at his home. They fell into conversation on Christian experience. This aged minister told how many years since he had found and been able to walk in conscious cleansing from all sin. The professor listened with interest, and when the old saint was through, he said to him: "Father, I have been seeking that blessing for ten years. I believe I have put all on the altar, and that I live with all on the altar; but I haven't received the power of sanctifying grace in my soul." Said the aged brother: "Do you want to receive it now?" The professor replied: "Yes." "Well," said the minister, "let us kneel down right here, and you may receive it now." One who has received full salvation, knows it may be received right away. The fully saved soul is very alert, and precipitous in its faith. They had been sitting side by side in the professor's parlor.

The professor was a little reluctant to believe that the struggle of ten years could end right away. He doubtless thought the old man very sanguine. But they knelt together. "Now," said the minister, "Professor, are you wholly given to God?" and with much tenderness and honesty of heart, he said: "I believe I am." "You have put all on the altar?" "Yes." "Well, Professor, the Lord says, 'The altar sanctifieth the gift;' is it true or not?" He dare not tempt God, and say it is not, and with a faltering, and almost coerced faith, he said, "It is true," and instantly the refining fire went through his soul.

The conscious acceptance of the Word of God as true to itself, by the soul, is characteristic of the witness of faith.

II. The conscious commitment of the saving work to Christ:

When the soul consciously relinquishes its own efforts to save itself, and puts itself to be saved into the hands of Him who came to save it, and does this so really to itself, that it dismisses all concern for its salvation; not that it feels that it is saved, but because it knows that it has committed itself unto him whose sole business is to redeem from all iniquity, it has the witness of faith.

Not long since, a gentleman, a comparative stranger to me, but who had reasonable evidence of my integrity, said to me: "I have been owing a gentleman in the town in which you live, seventy-five dollars. I want to pay it but cannot leave my home to do so. Will you take the money to him?" I said: "I will." He handed me the amount. When I took it, I saw an expression of relief come to his face, and he felt an evident satisfaction which showed that he counted his debt paid. He had committed to me the work of canceling the note held against him. He knew I would do it. It was in effect to him the payment of his debt. The burden was off his mind; he felt that his business integrity for fidelity in meeting his claims was vindicated. His conscious commitment to me of this business, brought him the rest which the witness of faith always insures.

He got clear of concern for its payment several hours before it was paid, because I took the care of its payment off him, which I could not have done if he had not confided in my word of promise to him. So, when the soul commits the concern of its salvation unto Him who is able to save unto the uttermost, then it begins to take up the triumphant shout which the witness of faith always inspires,

"Hallelujah' 'tis done: I believe on the Son I am saved by the blood of the crucified One."

This conscious commitment by the soul of its salvation to Christ is characteristic of the witness of faith.

III. A conscious act of trust by the soul.

The soul is conscious of its own voluntary acts. We know when a person or plan commands our confidence. We know when we believe. There may be much struggle in order for the soul to settle down and accept the evidence which solicits its faith; but when it passes from the attitude of distrust, or even questioning, to that of trust, it knows it. When the soul sets itself about to trust for salvation, the Adversary comes with his insinuations against, and contradictions of, the Word of the Lord; moreover, he seeks to divert the soul's attention from the glorious promises, the ample provisions, and mighty power of the gospel, to its own weakness, waywardness, and unworthiness, so that the soul must close its ears to the voice of Satan, and look steadily to Jesus, the author and finisher of its faith.

But when the contest is ended, and the soul has made up its mind to trust the sure word of the Lord, it becomes just as conscious that it believes as that it sees, or hears, or lives. Faith is an act to be performed. It is a thing to be done, and like any other act in which the mind is concerned, when it receives the light, so the heart knows when it receives Jesus-when it believes on the Son.

One evening, nine seeking hearts arose from an altar of prayer, burdened and unhappy because they had not accepted salvation on the Word of the Lord. They looked forlorn and sad. The congregation joined in singing that sweet salvation hymn,

'Tis the promise of God full salvation to give Unto him who on Jesus, his Son, will believe," accompanied by the faith inspiring chorus,

"Hallelujah! 'tis done: I believe on the Son; I am saved by the blood of the crucified One."

As its lines were successively repeated, first one, then another, of these seekers came into the witness of faith, and began in heart, and some of them with voice, to say, rejoicingly:

"Hallelujah! 'tis done."

What is done? "Why, 'I believe on the Son.' What then? "Why, 'I am saved by the blood of the crucified One.'"

Before all the stanzas had been sung through, eight out of the nine had experienced the witness of faith. One, a railroad engineer, had not come into the rest of faith. The pastor said to him: "Brother, when you make up your mind to believe on the Son, you will begin to sing-

"Hallelujah! 'tis done: I am saved by the blood of the crucified One."

But his mind was so intent on having a blessing and the witness, that he could not, for the time being, be led to an immediate act of trust. His vocation took him away from the services several days. About the third day after, the pastor met him on the street coming from his locomotive. As soon as he saw the pastor, he exclaimed:

"Hallelujah! 'tis done: I believe on the Son; I am saved by the blood of the crucified One."

His soul was happy in a conscious trust in Jesus, his precious Savior. He said: "Yesterday, while I was taking my train over my regular trip, at the rate of twenty miles an hour, it all came over me, Why not believe on the Son? and I did, and though traveling at such a rapid speed, salvation overtook me there and then, and ever since I have been singing in my heart:

"Hallelujah! 'tis done: I believe on the Son, I am saved"

Glory to the Lamb!

This glorious witness of faith to his soul was soon supplemented by the witness of the Holy Spirit itself. His reception of salvation was soon followed by his realization of salvation.

How glorious is the witness of faith! It is in us. This consciousness of faith is a light unto our path, and when every other light of experience is extinguished, this illuminates the soul, and still, it sings:

"Trusting thee, I cannot stray, I can never lose my way."

Glory to God! "He that believeth on the Son hath the witness in himself."

Chapter 5: Its Experience

I Peter 1: 5, 9: "In whom, though now ye see him not, yet believing, ye rejoice with joy unspeakable and full of glory: receiving the end of your faith, even the salvation of your souls."

The witness of faith is just as conscious an experience as is the witness of the Holy Spirit. It comprises emotions of joy, peace, and gladness peculiar to itself. There is a faith-feeling just as there is a fear-feeling or a love-feeling. There is no true faith without feeling. Who can confide in a friend without any emotion of pleasure? Or who can accept in good faith the promise of another, and not feel a gladness of heart? As Dr. Lowrey wrote some months since, in The Divine Life: "The truth is, faith is a matter of feeling." To speak of believing without feeling is very misleading; for where believing begins, feeling also begins. A man without any faith-feeling may begin to believe; but when he does so, he also begins to feel the emotions which accompany faith. Faith is all experience as well as an act of the soul, and the witness of faith is both the consciousness of all acts performed and of a feeling experienced. This faith-feeling is just as real as the feeling which is concomitant to the experience of the Holy Spirit's witness. And not only so, but in its own kind there is as great an intensity of emotion in the experience of faith as there is in the experience of the Holy Spirit's witness. "Joy in believing" and "joy in the Holy Ghost," though different forms of joy, may both be alike unspeakable and full of glory. When faith is immediate, lively and unwavering, it not only brings salvation and joy in believing, but more-joy unspeakable and full of glory. The experience of the witness of faith is most precious. The following are some of its most interesting phases:

I. A sense of rest

Faith always brings rest of soul. They who believe, do enter into rest. Faith and rest are Siamese twins; they are inseparable. When faith is wanting. rest is wanting; and when rest is wanting, faith is wanting. President Finney used to frequently say: "Whenever you get out of rest, you are out of faith." The witness of faith brings a rest to the soul from all fear as to its saving interest in Christ. Having consciously received the Lord Jesus as its Savior, it no longer fears. Faith is a complete antidote to fear. Faith is the stronger one which casts out the strong man, fear, from the soul. All fear of law, of judgment, of penalty, and of every other evil thing, departs, when faith possesses the heart. Faith emancipates from fear.

There comes also with the witness of faith a rest from the seeking or struggle for salvation. The pursuit is over; the faith that saves is realized; salvation is received; expectation is at an end; anticipation has become attainment. The impulse to weep and struggle and pray for salvation subsides. When President Finney alone, praying in great agony of soul, experienced justification by faith, there was such a cessation of mental anxiety and of the impulse to pray, that walking home, he was tempted to think that, instead of being converted, he had only fallen into indifference. But it was the true rest of faith that always marks the end of seeking and the beginning of receiving salvation. It is such a rest that all concern for salvation vanishes. The soul that believes on the Son of God has no concern about salvation.

Moreover, this rest of faith frees the seeking soul from anxiety about the witness of the Holy Spirit; for faith commits both the saving work and the witness of the same to Christ so implicitly that it can have no restless longing for either. I read, not long since, this sentence, which is a golden spiritual axiom: "In proportion as a seeking soul is anxiously concerned for the witness of the Holy Spirit, in that degree it is doubting." Sometimes, indeed most generally, the last bulwark of unbelief that surrenders to faith is to accept salvation on the Word of the Lord without the witness of the Holy Spirit, and to rejoice that the Holy Spirit in his own time and in his own way will attest the saving work that shall be wrought in us. A young man came to me in great trouble. I was just starting to my pulpit on Sabbath morning. He was weeping and was a very picture of distress. I could only talk with him a few minutes. He told me his trouble. I said to him: "I will fix matters so that your trouble will be at an end." I did not say when or how I would do it. He wiped away his tears; a restful expression took the place of the worried features he wore when he entered my door. I had done nothing; I had only promised to do something. He believed me, and rest came to his troubled heart. He left me within five minutes bright and happy. I attended to his case as soon as I could, and saved him from the trouble which threatened him, and did not see him again until two days afterward. I met him on the street. I supposed his first inquiry would be, "Have you attended to my case?" that he would want a witness that I had done what I had promised; but he conversed with me several minutes, and asked nothing about what I had promised, and was about to leave, when I said to him: "Your matter is all adjusted."

"O," said he: "I knew that was all right I had no anxiety about it, since you said you would attend to it." He had all this while been unconcerned about any assurance that I had done it; he had not worried himself about such an assurance, nor had he worried me about it. So, the soul, when it accepts God's promise of salvation by faith, rests from all concern about the witness of the Holy Spirit; it doesn't worry itself, nor does it worry the Lord about it. As long as the soul is fretting about the witness, and pestering the Lord about it, it has not yet the rest of faith; for faith brings rest from all such unnecessary anxiety, I said to a lady who had accepted Christ by faith for full salvation: "Have you the witness of the Spirit?" She instantly said: "No, and I don't care; for I know it will come." She had the witness of faith, and that earnest of the promised witness of the Holy Spirit was sufficient for her.

II. A sense of possession

Faith is an act of claiming, of receiving. It takes what is proffered in the promises of God's Word; so that with it there springs up in the heart a sweet sense of ownership, and the soul begins to say: "Jesus is mine," "I am saved."

Joshua was commanded of the Lord to say to the children of Israel: "Ye shall pass over this Jordan to possess the land which the Lord thy God giveth you to possess it." Then he added: "Every place where the sole of your foot shall tread upon, that I have given unto you." Wherever Judah should set his foot that should be his; where Benjamin should set his foot, that should be his. Each should get his inheritance by setting his foot upon it. Now, think you not, when either had set his foot upon a given territory, he did not instantly and instinctively feel, This is mine?

Think you not that he would have defended his proprietorship against every other contestant? And would he not have felt at once a joyful sense of ownership of the tract he had thus pre-empted? So when the soul sets the foot of its faith upon pardon or full salvation as promised to him, there does come to it immediately such a precious persuasion of possessorship as fills it with a gladness which cannot be quenched by any lack of further witness, or by any temptation of the adversary to think otherwise. The instant the footfall of faith is set upon the promise, the soul begins to sing: The witness of faith is always,

"And all its riches mine."

"It is done; I believe on the Son; I am saved by the blood Of the crucified One."

An old colored man, who had a marvelous experience in grace, was asked: "Daniel, why is it that you have so much peace and joy in religion?" "O Massa!" he replied, "I just fall flat on the exceeding great and precious promises, and I have all that is in them. Glory, Glory!" He who falls flat on the promises, feels that all the riches embraced in them are his.

III. A sense of satisfaction.

Faith is a state of satisfaction. Persons sometimes say: "I am trusting, but I am not satisfied." That is impossible for the soul that is trusting for salvation is satisfied with "salvation by promise," and anticipates soon "salvation by power." If your home were under order from the court to be sold tomorrow, to cancel a judgment against you for one thousand dollars, and you had no money wherewith to redeem it, and a friend should, tonight, present you with a note on the Bank of England for one thousand dollars, do you think you would say to him: "I am not satisfied?" Would you feel, I haven't any money! Would you not rather experience the sweetest satisfaction? and would you not joyfully tell your wife and children: I have one thousand dollars; our home is saved? Yet that banknote is only a piece of paper; it is neither silver nor gold; the judgment is still upon your home, but somehow that banknote commands so implicitly your confidence that you are most delightfully satisfied. So, when the soul accepts in like faith any one of Heaven's banknotes of promise as the pledge of either pardon, purity, or power, a satisfaction takes possession of the heart that is unspeakable and full of glory; for Heaven's bank of grace cannot fail, and Heaven's paper is payable at sight. The value of the witness of faith has been greatly underestimated in the instruction of seekers of salvation. It should be emphasized as the objective point in seeking salvation. The struggle of most seeking hearts is for the witness of the Holy Spirit, and in most cases, this is so prominent in their minds as to hinder them more than any other thing in attaining it. It is the vain struggle to have God do his work, which he will certainly do without our anxiety or struggle about it. The real struggle should be for the seeking heart to do its part; that is, to believe unto salvation, and so attain the witness of faith which always brings a glorious rest and satisfaction of soul. We have seen souls come into the joy of pardon or full salvation, receiving the witness of the Holy Spirit thereto. Then we have seen these in an hour, a day, or a week, doubting the divine work wrought in their hearts; some even casting away their confidence and forfeiting their pardon, or cleansing. The cause of this was evident. When their emotions subsided, the tempter came and said: "Where is your salvation? you have no feeling;" and not having clearly discerned that they were saved by faith, they concluded they were deceived, and lapsed into darkness. Suppose they had learned that "only trusting" they were saved; then when an abatement of the joy came which was concomitant to the witness of the Holy Spirit, they would have repelled the temptation of the adversary by simply singing, "I am trusting, Lord, in thee," and they would not only have retained the rest of faith, but there would doubtless have come a renewed and more powerful witness of the Holy Spirit. Here is a spiritual axiom that is invaluable: The witness of faith attained, the witness of the Holy Spirit always follows; and the witness of faith maintained, retains and increases the power of the witness of the Holy Spirit.

A man, in a meeting I held, had been very clearly and powerfully converted. It was a wonderful conversion, such as no one should ever doubt; but within three days I found him bordering on despair, walking in darkness, and about to conclude that he was not saved. The intensity of heart emotion, and the corresponding nervous excitement, which the first realization of saving grace brought, had subsided, and he feared that it had all been excitement and no salvation. I said to him: "Are you still given to God?" He replied: "Yes." "Have you ceased to trust Jesus to save you?" "O!" said he, "that was the way I was saved, wasn't it? I just trusted. O, I will trust on!" and instantly rest came again into his heart, and in a few moments the Holy Spirit's witness was renewed in great power to him, and ever since he has been a stable and growing Christian, and now walks in the blessing of perfect cleansing, through the blood of the Lamb, by faith. It is said, one reason why the work of conversion and entire sanctification under Mrs. Phoebe Palmer has such permanence in the hearts of those whom she led to Christ, was because she emphasized so constantly the faith that saves.

"Whosoever believeth shall not make haste." "Now may the God of hope fill you with all joy and peace in believing!"

Chapter 6: The Fulness of Faith: Its Characteristics

Acts vi, 5: "A man full of faith."

Faith is well defined to him who possesses it; it is but imperfectly apprehended until experienced. He who has faith in any degree, hungers and thirsts for it in a larger degree; a taste of faith makes the soul eager for a feast of it. Every believer has faith, but not every believer is full of faith; with much faith there may coexist much lack of faith. Therefore, Paul longed to see the faces of the brethren at Thessalonica, that he "might perfect that which was lacking in their faith." The soul may have saving faith, and still lack a fullness of faith. In this series of "FAITH PAPERS" we have hitherto been presenting the subject of saving faith; we now take up the subject of special faith, which, under various phases, is as clearly distinguished in the Scriptures from saving faith as saving faith is from unbelief.

Much of the misapprehension which exists respecting the nature of faith arises from confounding faith in its saving measure with faith in the measure of its fullness. SAVING FAITH is a voluntary act of the soul, by which it appropriates salvation THE FULLNESS OF FAITH is a state of the soul in which it apprehends divine and spiritual things; it is a temper of mind -- an entirely new fame of heart: it is faith shorn of none of its saving efficacy, graduated into the "substance of things hoped for and the evidence of thing not seen" by the baptism of the Holy Ghost in his indwelling presence received into the soul. Let us notice some of the characteristics of THE FULLNESS OF FAITH:

I.   A consciously exclusive confidence in God.

Having the fullness of faith, the soul continuously exclaims, under all circumstances, with the Psalmist, "Wait thou only upon God; for my expectation is from him;" it is such a vision and persuasion of God's almightiness, all-lovingness, and all-faithfulness as that the soul is given a set God-ward it will not look for help self-ward, man-ward, earth-ward, circumstance-ward, - or other-ward. Faith in an imperfect measure is often deluded by favorable circumstances or promising indications, only to be disappointed. I recall in my own early ministry how my immature faith was disappointed on one occasion in its hopes, because it unconsciously reposed on indications. A protracted meeting was begun; the attendance was large; general interest good; my heart prophesied to itself a glorious revival. But the interest evanesced; the results were meager. My faith had been misplaced. As I now know, I had great faith in the indications, and but little faith in God.

A noted evangelist taught me in a very abrupt way a lesson of faith. I had been chosen to welcome him to the city where he was to labor. I met him on his arrival at the depot; introduced myself to him, when he at once informally said to me: "Have you faith in God?" I replied: "Our preparatory services have been good; the indications are favorable." Instantly he rejoined: "We can't depend on good meetings, favorable indications, or anything of that kind. Have you faith in God?" Then as I came to think of it, I found that I had much faith in the auspicious meetings already held, and in the coming evangelist, but very little faith in God.

The soul that is full of faith never becomes confounded by unconscious dependence upon apparent encouragements. Neither will discouragements dismay it. Oppositions, adversities, difficulties, do not enter into its calculations. It believes fully that all things are possible to him that believeth. It anticipates revivals in the face of prevalent deadness; expects victory where opposition is the most formidable; and keeps in heart where providences are the most disheartening. The fact is, a soul full of faith can't be discouraged, because it knows it shall not be disappointed. It shouts for what is to be done, even when, to human appearance, there is no hope of success. It says, "We are fully able to go up," though the rabble of unbelief clamors: "We can't." It utters the victorious hallelujahs which bring the walls of every frowning Jericho into the dust.

A pastor, who had not yet entered into the fullness of faith, closed a weekly prayer meeting, heart-sunken with discouragement, because of the few present and the unpromising outlook for the Church, when a good brother present came up to him and said "What a good meeting we had tonight! The Lord is going to revive his work." That was the outlook of faith in its fullness. A pastor went to his field of labor; everything was unpromising; religion was in great decline. His wife said: "There can be no success here." His reply was: "Faithful is he who hath promised, who also will do it." That faith was honored in a most wonderful ingathering of souls and a great quickening of the Church a few months later. Faith in its fullness is,

"A faith that shines more bright and clear, When tempests rage without, That when in danger knows no fear, In darkness feels no doubt."

That sister most nearly discovered the secret of the Rev. Thomas Hanson's power as an evangelist, who said: "He is a knot of faith. A man full of faith."

A man full of faith is a man of God. He has a sustained conviction that God cannot be unfaithful, and has an impressive sense that he is, and that he is rewarder of those who trust him.

II. A consciously vivid apprehension of Christ.

Having the fullness of faith, Christ is to the soul, the Son of God indeed. The divinity of the Lord Jesus Christ becomes a spiritual verity, rather than a doctrinal conception. He who is full of faith cannot be a Unitarian, for he knows by spiritual cognition that Jesus is Lord. The soul on the heights of the fullness of faith falls in adoring love at the feet of Jesus, and exclaims "My Lord and my God," as never before. The sacrificial work of Christ receives under the illumination of faith in its fullness a new interpretation to the heart. The mystery of the cross becomes the glory of the soul.

The blood of the cross is exalted into infinite worth; it is seen as the sole ground of reconciliation, justification, sanctification, and eternal redemption; it is recognized not as a part, but as the whole of the atoning work; not as its symbol, but as its substance. The blood has wondrous significance to one who is full of faith; he sings of it with a sense of appreciation greatly augmented over that which he felt the hour he first believed.

That sweet apostrophe so often sung,

"O the blood, the precious blood, Which Jesus shed for me!":

thrills his heart with raptures that are inexpressible. The substitutional propitiatory significance of the death of Christ is no longer a dogma, but a felt truth. Moreover, the name of Jesus becomes freighted with a power that is measureless; it is seen as:

"The name high over all."

as the prevailing element of successful prayer; as the mediatorial channel of all communion and communication between God and man as the true Jacob's ladder which joins earth and heaven, and this Christian life into a Bethel-a house of God. Christ becomes the Alpha and Omega, the first and the last, the all and in all to the soul which has come into the fullness of faith. So realized is Jesus to the soul in sensible glory that it exclaims:

"O could I speak the matchless worth; O could I sound the glories forth, Which in my Savior shine, I'd soar, and touch the heavenly strings, And vie with Gabriel while he sings, In notes almost divine!"

I once called upon a lady who had gone through deep waters of sorrow. When I met her, she had not been inside of a church for four years, though a Christian. The death of her husband had so saddened her by the peculiar circumstances under which it had occurred, that she could not summon courage to take her accustomed place in the house of God. Besides, the shadow of sorrow rested so deeply upon her heart that she had kept, all through those four years, lights burning every night in every room of her house, not out of superstition, but because she felt that natural darkness, superadded to the darkness of her sorrow, was more than she could bear. I said to her: "Jesus will help you and comfort you." She replied petulantly: "You ministers say Jesus will be this and Jesus will be that to the soul, but he has been nothing to me in this sorrow." I saw she was not in condition to be talked with much. She was holding on to Jesus as her Savior but had not embraced him as her Comforter. She was made the subject of special prayer by a few to whom her case was reported. A few weeks after wards she came to one of our morning meetings. I was almost startled when I saw her enter the door. A few minutes after the meeting began, she arose, and said in almost an exclamatory tone; "It is true, it is true! Jesus can help a broken heart! O, he came into my soul yesterday, and I blew out all the lights last night, and my soul and my home are now brighter than when all were burning." When she opened her heart and received the Comforter, there sprang up in her heart a fullness of faith which realized Jesus to her in all his "matchless worth." Such faith is the soul's Mount of Transfiguration, where it beholds in beatific visions the glories which in our Savior shine. Dear reader, may you allow the Holy Spirit to translate you to this heavenly place; for once there you will desire to build tabernacles, and will sing:

"Here I should forever stay, Weep and gaze myself away."

III. A consciously higher appreciation of God's Word.

The Bible is an infallible book to the soul that is full of faith. It is then received as a divine revelation, as the very Word of God. It becomes a volume all instinct with holy inspiration. The plenary inspiration of the Holy Scripture passes from being a merely doctrinal conception into a spiritual apprehension. He who has come into a fullness of faith drops all questioning and quibbling as to the complete inspiration and divine authority of the Scriptures; their very enigmas, difficulties, and obscurities are accepted as significant; and what is incomprehensible in them is believed even more fully than what is clearly understood. The fullness of faith not only accepts the Bible an inspired book, but it also renders it an illuminated book. It reads it by a new light and sees in it new meaning. The soul, full of faith, sings:

"Holy Bible, Book divine, Precious treasure, thou art mine!"

The Bible, hitherto uninteresting, becomes a supreme delight.

Once in my ministry, a lady came to me who was a very creditable worker in my Church, and a converted woman, and she said to me: "I don't love to read the Bible. I haven't a relish for it. I find that I prefer to read the magazines and the best authors and current papers. There must be something wrong. I know I ought to love the Bible." I said: "There is something wrong. You need that baptism of the Holy Spirit that will unseal the book and illuminate its pages so that your soul will exclaim, 'How I love Thy law!' " About two months after she came to me and said: "O, the Bible is a changed book to me now! O, it is a new book, such a precious book! I only wish I had more hours in which to linger over its pages!" I asked her what had transformed it so wonderfully to her? She replied: "I went with it open before me on my knees one day, and I said: 'Give me, Lord, a heart to love and delight in thy Word,' and there came to me such a view of its truth, and such a sense of its divine origin, that my heart was filled with a completeness of faith in it, and ever since it has been a glorious enjoyment to me."

The fullness of faith comprises such an immediate confidence in God, such an apprehension of Christ, and such a full reception of the Bible as the Word of God, as gives to Christian experience an effectiveness, enjoyment, and completeness that saving faith alone does not compass. Have we this baptism of faith? The triumphant experience of Stephen is not beyond the reach of every believer. He was "a man full of faith." We, too, may be full of faith.

"Lord give us such a faith as this, And then, whate'er may come, We'll taste, e'en here, the hallowed bliss Of an eternal home."

Chapter 7: Its Effects

Heb. xi, 33: "Who through faith wrought righteousness, obtained promises, stopped the months of lions."

Faith is always effectual: it eventuates in results; it brings something to pass. What it brings to pass, however, depends upon its aim. If it claims pardon or purity or power, according as it is, so shall it be done unto it. To say, "Trust in the Lord and care nothing for results," is misleading. That would not be faith at all, for it belongs to faith to believe for something; it must anticipate results. Faith is always accompanied by effects. Some effects are promised to faith in its saving exercise, and other effects are promised to it in the exercise of its fullness. The effects possible to the one are different from those possible to the other Saving faith compasses pardon, regeneration, witness of adoption, and entire sanctification; while faith in its fullness compasses a range of spiritual experiences and states not possible to lower measures of faith. Faith in its fullness brings to pass conversions, and results in the domain of personal consciousness which would not otherwise transpire.

Let us consider the effects of the fullness of faith in two respects,

I. Its achievements.

It renders the personality of the man who has it effective for God; his finite capabilities are raised to superhuman power; it endows him with power for spiritual results. Barnabas was full of faith and of power. Power is the inseparable concomitant of fullness of faith; they are hemispheres of the same globe. The simplest definition of power is faith in God.

He who is full of faith is mighty through God. Deprive D. L. Moody of this faith, and all his native personal force would achieve nothing in the great work of evangelization; he would be powerless.

Nothing other than John Wesley's superadded faith made his scholarship, culture, and marked individuality so effective and far-reaching for good as they have proved. This fullness of faith empowers all religious activities: it gives weight to our words of testimony, exhortation, and instruction; freighted with it they carry a spiritual avoirdupois which may break stolid hearts into penitence or exert a spiritual force that may lift souls up to God. With it, a sentence often achieves more than a sermon without it.

An aged Christian lady visited a worldly, irreligious man at his home, and said to him: "You ought not to lose your soul." Just what he had heard before in sermons and exhortations; but as they fell from the lips of that saintly woman, freighted with a great faith, they weighed," as he said, upon his heart so that he could not eat or sleep or work, or do aught else, until he had given his heart to Christ. Mr. Finney was a man of such faith that his words of reproof and appeal went in an airline to the heart, producing immediate impression in the soul. He met at one time a worldly young woman, who belonged to the family in which he was a guest, coming out of the Church at the close of one of his impressive services. He said to her: "Where are you going?" She replied: "Home." "Yes," rejoined Mr. Finney, "to your long home." Her countenance fell, she grew sober, walked silently and tremblingly to her home, and when Mr. Finney arrived, she lay upon the floor in an agony of distress on account of her lost condition. I know a lady whose words in ordinary conversation have a spiritual edge which faith alone can put to language. Sitting one evening in the midst of a social company, she began to speak so impressively, in a natural and unpretentious way, of the Lord's dealings with her soul that some began to weep. Noticing it, she modestly asked the privilege of praying. When they arose, a husband and wife had found the joy of a restored salvation, and a young lady had been enriched with the pearl of great price. Her words had been words of faith. Such a faith imparts an effectiveness to pulpit utterances, home counsels, and Sabbath-school instruction, as they cannot have without it. The fullness of faith empowers the life of the child of God; it makes it tell; it invests it with a quietness of manner, a sweetness of spirit, and an earnestness of demeanor that is more influential in winning souls to Christ than any other thing. There was a young man who had become infatuated with the deceits of Ingersollism. He thought he had come to a full acceptance of its errors and had about concluded that the Church was nothing to be respected, the Bible a human invention, and religion a mere fancy. Just about this time he went to write at the same desk in an office where there stood opposite him a devoted young man, full of faith and the Holy Ghost. There they stood facing each other, pushing busily their pens for several months. Occasionally the young skeptic would flaunt out his reproaches upon Christianity, and his infidel objections. His godly associate refrained from any sharp retorts, and declined all controversy, but kept his soul so full of faith that he wore a bright face, carried a good spirit, and maintained an irreproachable life. One evening this skeptical young man fell in with the pastor of the Church to which his religious business companion belonged. As they walked together this disciple of Ingersoll said very abruptly: "I have made up my mind to join your Church." The pastor, much surprised, said: "I am glad of it. Come next Sabbath and I will receive you; and now tell me what has changed your mind." "O," said he, "I have been writing for several months at a desk with a young man, a member of your Church. He never gets out of humor; he always seems so happy, and he is so kind that he has burned all my infidelity out of me, and I want just what he has, and I believe he has religion." The next Sabbath he united with the Church and is now a happy and useful Christian. That Christian young man lived a life of faith, and it told. The fullness of faith always enables the Christian to live a spiritually energized life for God. The works and labors of love in Christian life are multiplied and enlarged under the power of a fullness of faith. It originates greater things, plans larger enterprises, inaugurates bolder endeavors, and compasses richer results than faith in its minor measures. Its works for the salvation of men are wonderful; it always abounds in the work of the Lord. It carries forward a sustained work of prayer. The man full of faith is pre-eminently a man of prayer; he, like Payson, is audacious in prayer; asks large things, and asks with a boldness whose demands God never denies. Said one who listened to one of the simple prayers of that prince of faith, Bishop William Taylor, "He isn't backward in asking the Lord for great things." No man of faith is. Success crowns the man full of faith; he doesn't fail; his labor is not in vain; whatsoever he doeth prospers; fruit appears; results follow. The fullness of faith accomplishes the grand achievements of transforming its possessor into a power for God, and of precipitating divine movements in the Church, the world, and human hearts, which eventuate in marked results in the salvation of souls.

II. Its experiences.

All the effects of faith within the domain of personal consciousness are real and precious. The conscious experiences which result from saving faith, such as a sense of pardon, adoption, and a new life, are not to be undervalued; yet there remain coexistent with these disagreeable elements of consciousness, such as doubts, fears, and clouds. These commingle with the peace, joy, and light of the' converted soul, so that it often sings:

"E'en the rapture of pardon is mingled with fears. And the cup of rejoicing with sadness and tears."

Its enjoyments are, at best, variable. The particular improvement in the realm of experience which the fullness of faith brings is that it clears the skies of the soul, disperses its shadows, and secures to it a sustained light, warmth, and enjoyment in God. There are several new elements of experience which it ushers in.

I. Full assurance.

It so fully persuades the soul of its acceptance with God, makes it so conscious of his indwelling presence, and so assures the soul of the verity of spiritual things, that the soul walks in the light and sings,

"Not a cloud doth arise To darken my skies."

Doubts vanish; their hideous specters never even flit across the soul; and the experience of the seraphic Faber becomes verified to the heart:

"I know not what it is to doubt; My heart is always gay."

The soul stands on the solid ground of conscious certainty respecting its salvation and hope. It walks now by faith. Some speak often of walking by faith as though it were a rough, dark way. They say: "I have many doubts, much darkness, no joy, but I am walking by faith." By no means are they. Faith's way is not such; it is a cloudless way, a smooth way, a joyous way. The way that is cloud-cast and doubt-strewn is the way of sight. The fullness of faith is a vision of soul, where its eye, as it sweeps the horizons of time and eternity,

"Reads its title clear To mansions in the skies," rejoices in hope, walks above the world and sin, and to it "The invisible appears, And God is seen by mortal sight"

The exclamation of one when faith's full orb had risen within his soul was, "Lo, what a witness! Clearer than that of my adoption it is a perfect globe of assurance."

2. Freedom from fear is another new phase of experience of soul which attends the fullness of faith. The dread of duty which haunts so many Christian lives, and which paralyzes the soul's sensibilities for enjoying God, quits the soul. Crosses become delights, service joy. Faith in its fullness emancipates the soul from the bondage of doing duty in the dread of it and brings it the liberty of doing duty in the love of it. This is accompanied by a freedom from the fear of God's' will. The chief reason why so many Christians hesitate to offer themselves "living sacrifices unto God," is that they fear to say, "Thy will be done." They fear that he may choose some suffering or disappointment or persecution or bereavement for them. But the soul full of faith adores God's sweet will; it is so persuaded of the divine all-lovingness, that he will not choose for it what is not best, as that it has no concern about what his will is concerning it. The bondage of dreading a loving Father's will is supplanted by the liberty of delighting in it. This embraces, also, no fear for the future. Said a Christian woman: "I have grace sufficient for the present, but I don't believe I could endure the trials and temptations some have, should they come to me." Had she been "full of faith" she would have been quiet from the fear of evil. The soul full of faith fears neither coming age or service or death. It lives in no fear of backsliding or spiritual decline, or fruitless years to come; its confidence is like Paul's: "I am persuaded that he is able to keep that which I have committed unto him." A Christian woman was in the habit of saying in the presence of her saintly colored servant, who was always happy: "Dinah, suppose this should happen, or that should come to you, some great sorrow, accident, or misfortune." "Why, missus," said Dinah, "I never sposes anything; its your sposes that make you so miserable. I knows all things work together for good to dem what loves de Lord, and that makes me happy all de time." Dinah was full of faith. Such a soul never supposes anything about the future, and so rejoices in hope.

3. Heavenly mindedness is another new element of experience in the soul full of faith.

Heavenly mindedness is a state, not a mere emotion of soul. The heart becomes possessed of heavenly thoughts and feelings. It lives on a celestial altitude of experience in the midst of pressing duties, cares, and perplexities. It is an experience akin to what some saints have realized during long periods of decline, as they anticipated their early translation to heaven. Said Mrs. Professor Lacroix, days before her death, "I am done with earth; I have begun to live in heaven." Thus, by the power of a fullness of faith, the soul, not waiting for the near approach of death, may be lifted into an experience where it begins to live the heavenly life while yet in the body. Then, as one has beautifully written: "It goes to heaven before it gets there locally. God transfers his kingdom and glory to the heart, making it a province of the land of light in advance. The whole realm of its inner being is annexed to the heavenly empire, and its citizenship is transferred from earth to the heavenly city." O glorious, wondrous faith, which enables us to know,

"Our heaven begun below!"

Dear reader, may the Lord lead you to this fullness of faith, so that having your conversation in heaven you may exultantly sing,

"Yet onward I haste to the heavenly feast: That indeed is the fullness, but this is the taste, And this I shall prove, till with joy I remove To the heaven of heavens in Jesus' love."

Chapter 8: Its Attainment

Acts xi, 24: "Full of the Holy Ghost and of faith."

The fullness of faith is a work of the Holy Spirit. Therefore, when the apostle Paul sets forth the fruit of the Spirit, he puts into the precious cluster faith. Now, since the Spirit himself, in fullness, is only given to believers, after they have exercised saving faith (that is, it is a Post-conversion experience), therefore, the faith which flows from his indwelling must be some enlargement and enrichment of faith which does not belong to it in its initial character. Faith, in its saving measure, is faith with hands and feet unloosed, yet with eyes that are darkened and wings that are bound: it is a clinging chrysalis -- it neither sees nor soars. But faith in its fullness is faith with eyes wide open, and wings unbound. Faith never reaches its fullness until it transmigrates from an exercise into a state of soul, until it can apprehend, as well as appropriate, the things which are freely given it of God. When faith, without losing any of its saving virtue, by the power of the Holy Ghost in us becomes the substance of things hoped for, and the evidence of things not seen, it has reached its majority, it is full grown. The process for the attainment of the fullness of faith differs from that for the attainment of faith in its saving efficacy, because they differ in experience. Saving faith is a thing done by us, a conscious, voluntary act by which the soul accepts salvation; the fullness of faith is a state wrought in us by the baptism of the Holy Ghost. Being a grace wrought in us, it must be definitely sought and received as any other grace is obtained. Two things are very essential to the soul's attainment of the fullness of faith, it must know the source and the antecedents of this experience.

I. Its source.

The baptism of the Holy Ghost is the cause, and fullness of faith the effect. The fullness of the Holy Spirit implanted in the soul is the perennial fountain whence proceeds the ceaseless stream of fullness of faith. Barnabas was full of the Holy Ghost and consequently full of faith. When the Pentecostal grace is come, faith in its fullness has come. All lack of faith in true believers is the result of not having the baptism of the Holy Ghost. The gift of the Holy Ghost is to be distinguished from the ordinary operations of the Holy Spirit in awakening, regeneration, and adoption; it is His personal indwelling in the soul. When he has thus possessed the soul as a refiner, he purges away the dross of native unbelief from the heart; as an illuminator, he reveals Jesus as the author and finisher of faith; and as an empowerer, he spiritually energizes the soul to apprehend all the fullness of God in the promises of his Word. The fullness of the Holy Spirit himself received into the soul is the source of all fullness; not a grace of the Spirit can exist there in its fullness without his indwelling presence. Fullness of joy, fullness of love, fullness of faith, all in here in the fullness of the Holy Spirit. Faith cannot be trained into the stature of fullness. The fullness of faith is a product of the baptism of the Holy Ghost. Hence the early Church gave great attention, as a desideratum to the new converts, that they should be filled with the Holy Ghost. Therefore, we have in the Acts of the Apostles numerous records of individuals and of multitudes who received the anointing. Philip, the evangelist, had no sooner secured the conversion of hundreds in Samaria than the apostles hastened thither to impart the gift of the Holy Ghost. So that the fullness of faith became then a common, instead of an unusual, experience. Stephen was full of faith and the Holy Ghost. Saul of Tarsus, after his conversion to God on the Damascus road, under the instruction of a humble disciple, Ananias, was filled with the Holy Ghost; and there began his wonderful career of faith, of which, as life went on, he could say:

"The life I now live I live by the faith of the Son of God;" and when it was closing could triumphantly exclaim: "I have kept the faith." Now men and women get converted, live in Church for years, and do not so much as know whether there be any Holy Ghost as a source of a fullness of faith, This grace of faith, being a work of the Holy Spirit, bears his divine imprint. It is a spirit of faith; the soul is pervaded by its inspirations; it enters into all its states, experiences, and activities. The whole life has an air of faith; it is repose to the manner, confidence in the tone, steadiness in the demeanor. It is a spontaneous activity of the heart. Faith is no longer self-operated, but divinely operated. What is written comes to pass: "I will put my Spirit within you and cause you to walk in my statutes." The causative power of the Holy Spirit dwelling in us enables the soul to trust without effort or dint of will. The volitional becomes absorbed in the affectional emotions of the heart. Faith now works by love; believing becomes automatic -- it believes itself.

Faith is no more a task or wonder. To some it seems marvelous to have faith, but he who has operative in him the power of the Holy Ghost thinks it marvelous not to believe. The strain of faith is removed, and it is so easy to believe. More still, faith becomes, under the power of the Spirit, a sustained movement of soul. The Holy Spirit dwelling in the soul is a tremendous mainspring of feeling, thinking, and willing, coiled up in the center of spiritual life, to which every wheel of grace is attached, keeping it in continuous motion. This mainspring can't run down; its energies are eternal. Neither can the faith which it operates run down. So that faith in its fullness is not a fitful, wavering, and evanescent, but a prolonged, unabated, ceaseless experience of soul. The manifoldness of faith under the power of the Spirit is glorious; it is adequate to such a variety of wants, and compasses such a wide range of blessings; all things are possible to it, strength, consolation, wisdom. God withholds from it no good thing. Moreover, it is available. We have it. Let emergencies, crises, unexpected trials, providences, or duties arise, and it is on hand. So many of God's children have to work up faith for every new demand. If sorrow comes, they have to tug and toil for faith to bear it; if some new responsibility or service is thrust upon them, they have a severe struggle to get faith for it. So ministers and Churches squander a large part of the time given to special revival effort in getting faith for it.

But when the fullness of faith is had we have faith for every occasion, duty, and work; when the service or sorrow comes, the faith for it is at hand. The baptism of the Holy Spirit imparts to the soul full salvation; this removes the inherent unbelief, unspiritualness, and moral darkness of the soul, out of which arise the doubts, the fears, and the unrest which attend an immature faith, and which constitute the disabilities that render faith feeble and fitful.

There are those who desire faith -- great faith -- but who do not desire as well heart-purity, the only soil that can yield a fullness of faith. The kingdom of God in full salvation is a spiritual unit; it is indivisible. He who wants, its joy or its faith must take the entire kingdom. Receiving it, the soul becomes rich toward God: rich in faith, rich in love, rich in all goodness.

The grace of full salvation is not merely one of many manifestations of the Holy Spirit; it is not a blessing from the Holy Spirit, but the baptism of the Holy Spirit, comprehending his personal, conscious incoming into the soul, cleansing it from its sinward tendency, filling it with all the fullness of God, and imparting to it a fullness of faith, of love, and of power. It is more than a blessing. Said an excellent woman not long since who had found full salvation: "I have been getting blessings for years from the Lord; but this is more and better than they all." The fullness of faith and the fullness of love are not seriatim ingraftings upon the soul's experience but are scions of the one implanted tree of life, the Holy Spirit indwelling in the soul. Hence to seek a fullness of faith, exclusive of the sanctifying and enduing baptism of the Holy Ghost, is to limit the Holy One of Israel. He never imparts his graces without imparting himself. The soul that cries,

"Come, Holy Spirit, Heavenly Dove, With all thy quickening powers,"

will get the Holy Spirit himself, and in him will find all the fullness of faith.

II. Its Antecedents.

1. An unequivocal experience of saving faith.

There are no possibilities of faith in its higher degrees without saving faith attained and maintained. To renounce or undervalue saving faith, renders the fullness of faith impossible: "For we are partakers of Christ, if we hold the beginning of our confidence steadfast unto the end." Fullness of faith is saving faith expanded by the power of the Holy Ghost until it sweeps vast areas of divine blessing beyond the range of saving grace. George Muller, the founder of the Bristol orphanages, says he finds no difference in kind between the faith by which he trusts Christ to save his soul, and that by which he trusts God to feed, clothe, and shelter two thousand orphans. It is only saving faith given a wider range. Faith in its saving virtue is the germ faith in its fullness is the fruit. There must be first the blade of saving faith, then the ear of fullness of faith. The believer who would attain the grace of faith in its fullness must cry out: "Lord, I believe; help thou mine unbelief."

2. The consecration of saving faith to God.

An indispensable antecedent to the attainment of a fullness of faith is to put the talent of saving faith on the altar of God, as one of the powers of the soul made alive to him, to be transformed by the renewing of the Holy Ghost into a stature of fullness.

That faith by which the convert, or babe in Christ, feebly clings to the cross -- a faith so weak that it barely brings the peace of pardon, consecrated to God may transmigrate suddenly from a faith that saves into a faith which brings full assurance and a glorious apprehension of things not seen. Saving faith given to God unfolds into a fullness of faith.

3. The exercise of saving faith.

Saving faith is the only spiritual capability whose exercise can bring the fullness of faith. The faith which claims Christ as a Savior has only to receive him as the Baptizer with the Holy Ghost, and, lo! the promise of the Father descends; faith bursts into unclouded vision; its perfectness is come.

There are many who sigh over their infantile, weak, wavering faith, who, would they but use it in laying hold of some such promise as "How much more will your Heavenly Father give the Holy Spirit to them that ask him," would find it lifted into power and glory. By faith, "faith's increase we claim."

Dear reader, may the Lord perfect that which is lacking in your faith, "Spirit of Faith, come down: Reveal the things of God."

Chapter 9: The Gift of God

I Cor. xii, 9: "To another faith by the same Spirit."

The Bible treats of a phase of faith differing from both faith in its saving exercise and faith in its fullness; this it very properly designates "the gift of faith." When Paul enumerates the gifts sovereignly bestowed upon believers in the twelfth chapter of I Corinthians, the gift of faith is prominent in the list. The gift of faith operates in spheres which are not available to saving faith or to the fullness of faith; it apprehends results which only the supernatural illuminations of the Holy Spirit reveal to the soul as possible to faith. Without such a supernatural revelation the existence and exercise of charismatic faith, or the gift of faith, is impossible.

There is a gift of faith; it has not been withdrawn from God's people; it, like other manifestations of himself, the selfsame Spirit worketh in them who believe, as hitherto. Several features of the gift of faith may be profitably considered.

I. Its office.

The gift of faith is a divinely inwrought assurance given the soul that God will do in, for, or by the person upon whom it is bestowed, certain apprehended results, and this persuasion is so indubitable that it becomes the very substance of the things desired, and the very evidence (or proof), the conclusive testimony of the things not seen (not verified). Hence this faith is vital in certain of its relations. It is an indispensable qualification for the execution of some divine order by the person upon whom it is bestowed.

1. This gift is the indispensable accompaniment of the divine missions to which God appoints men.

When God calls one to the work of evangelist, teacher, prophet, or healer, he accompanies it with such an endowment of faith upon the soul as that the fruit of evangelism, teaching, prophecy, or healing shall appear. This gift attends such only in their divine callings and is effective only for their legitimate work. Sometimes the range of this endowment of faith is narrow, limited to only one phase of results, with one evangelist to the conversion of sinners, as with Philip of Samaria and Thomas Harrison of today; with E. P. Hammond to the conversion of children chiefly; with another to the sanctification of believers principally, as Dr. Sheridan Baker; with Miss Sarah Smiley, to teaching alone; with George Muller, to building orphanages; with Dr. Cullis to faith cures; with Francis Murphy, to reform inebriates. The divine call is the pledge of the divine anointing of faith for its work.

2. It is the indispensable antecedent of supernatural results in nature and mind through human agency.

The birth of Isaac in the ordinary course of nature was impossible. Many years after Abraham had believed the covenant promise of God by which he obtained justification, God appeared unto him; talked with him; promised him a son by Sarah and called his name Isaac. By this revelation of the Almighty God, Abraham is persuaded that what he has promised he is able to perform. He received the gift of faith, gave glory to God, and laughed outright from the delight of assurance which illuminated his soul. According to this faith, divinely imparted to him, it was done unto him. The miracle of the incarnation was through faith. The angel Gabriel being sent of God, came to a devout Galilean damsel residing at Nazareth; he saluted her: "Hail! thou art highly favored; the

Lord is with thee." Troubled in mind by the sudden appearance of this seraphic visitant, and his strange salutation, she is assured and comforted by a second message: "Fear not; thou hast found favor of the Lord. Thou shalt bring forth a son, and shalt call his name Jesus." This supernatural manifestation irresistibly persuaded her that it was the divine purpose that she should be the mother of the Lord. She consented to the mission, saying: "Be it unto me according to thy word." A divinely wrought faith possessed her heart. The divine Benedictus from the lips of Elizabeth, under the power of the Holy Ghost, confirmed it, saying: "Blessed is she that hath believed that there shall be a fulfillment of the things spoken to her from the Lord." Then breaks forth the shout of Mary's Spirit. imparted faith in the inspired Magnificat, "My soul doth magnify the Lord," etc., jubilant with all the anticipations which had their wondrous realization in the Advent. God gave Mary faith for this mission, and according to her faith it was done unto her. When God would make Ananias an agent for the salvation of Saul of Tarsus, he appears to him in a vision in the person of the ascended Lord, speaks to him, commissions him, discloses to him Saul's state of heart, silences his fears, assures him of the persecutor's true conversion, and of the divine purpose to make Saul a chosen vessel. All this brings the heart of Ananias into a sure confidence that the work committed to him shall not fail. He went; he succeeded; he witnessed the salvation of the great apostle to the Gentiles. So, it is ever: when God would have an extraordinary work achieved, or some unusual event transpire which is not according to the observed course of nature or mind, he works into some heart the supernatural persuasion that he will do this thing to, for, or by him.

These Scriptural citations are given only as samples of how, in like manner, God now sometimes imparts this gift of faith to his humblest disciples, enabling them to effect results, secure deliverances, promote revivals, and to do other mighty works.

Miss Sarah Smiley had been long an invalid; one day it came to her: "The Lord is thy healer!" It came so irresistibly that her heart responded, "Even so, Lord;" it was faith, for her healing. The next day she arose from her bed, grew stronger day by day, and has ever since been a successful evangelist.

A wife was impressed while praying to ask for the preservation and salvation of her husband, who was an officer on a Mississippi River steamer, then distant from home. The assurance of faith came that her desire was granted. The day following a telegram came to her that the steamer had burned, and that her husband had perished. She read it, folded it up, and said to the friend who delivered it: "It is not so; he is saved from the flames and the waves, and shall be from his sins." A few days after, he arrived home, was soon converted, and lived for many years, a praise in the Church.

Mr. Finney had visited a place to hold revival services. He was the guest of an excellent Christian woman. After he had held the first service, he determined to leave; his hostess urged him to stay, but he said he would leave. She then said: "Well, if you do go, God will send a revival anyhow." Mr. Finney stayed, and a most wonderful revival followed. She had the gift of faith for a revival. A young lady, backslidden in heart, filled with skeptical notions, reluctantly accompanied her godly father to church one night. Her mother in enfeebled health remained at home. While engaging in prayer, she was drawn out in supplication for her daughter's restoration to divine favor; while on her knees, an assurance of faith was given her that her daughter should not come home without being saved. Lo! when she returned home, she reported how the Lord had restored unto her the joy of salvation! The gift of faith is antecedent to and promotive of all such results as lie beyond the range of the blessings of grace promised to saving faith, and the experience of faith in the measure of its fullness,

3. It is the source of the prayer of faith.

That which is called in the Scriptures "the prayer of faith" springs out of the endowment of faith. The soul, becoming supernaturally assured by the Holy Spirit through the Word that it is God's will to do certain things by, for, or to it, instantly takes up prayer for that thing. What are often spoken of in Christian life as special answers to prayer, are those things given which were asked for when the soul was lifted into an assurance that God would grant those very things. The asking was prompted by the assurance of faith that had been given.

II. Its Order.

The gift of faith like every other gift of the Holy Spirit as a special endowment is inferior to the graces of the Spirit; for the apostle supposes it possible "to have all faith so as to remove mountains," and yet be destitute of love, the very substance of Christian experience. Indeed, he teaches that if endowed only with the gift of faith, "I am nothing." Several things suggest the inferiority of the gift of faith to the grace of faith in its saving exercise and the measure of its fullness.

1. The gift of faith is not obligatory.

The Scriptures nowhere enjoin that the soul must have faith to remove mountains, or heal diseases, or work miracles. Such faith is not essential in order to please God. It is indeed rather the reward of pleasing him than a requirement for pleasing him. "He that cometh to God [for salvation] must believe that he is, and that he is the rewarder of them that diligently seek him." "He that believeth not [unto salvation] is condemned already."

These and other passages teach that saving faith as a voluntary act of the soul, or the fullness of faith as a gracious state of the heart, is obligatory. The gift of faith is not optional, hence not obligatory. The holiest saint cannot have it when he wills. It is neither commanded of us, nor at our command. The Holy Spirit divideth (apportioneth) it to every man (in Christ) severally as he wills, and that which is conferred upon one by divine sovereign endowment is not obligatory. The grace of faith is not an endowment and is therefore a requirement. The possession of the grace of faith is a duty; the gift of faith is not. No one feels condemnation if he have not faith for the healing of his body, or any other supernatural result; but he does experience condemnation if he does not believe the record which God hath given concerning his Son for the salvation of his soul.

2. The gift of faith is not a constant experience.

It is not an abiding manifestation of the Holy Spirit; it is transient, variable, occasional. It is not given once for all, for ail things, and in all degrees. Paul had it for the healing of the father of Publius and others on the Island of Melita, but not for the restoration of Trophimus, whom he left behind at Melitum. "But now abideth faith [the grace of faith], hope, charity [love]; "that is, these are the staple graces -- the permanent experiences of Christian character. Whosoever believeth (present tense, meaning, begins to believe and continues to believe) shall be saved; that is, saving faith as a habit of the soul and the fullness of faith as a gracious state of the heart are the constant and not the variable qualities of Christian life. He who finds himself without the faith which brings marvelous things to pass may continue to rejoice, if he still have the grace of faith. But he who finds the faith which brings salvation wanting may well repine; for

"Its work will not be done, Till we the crown obtain."

3. The gift of faith is not essential to salvation or Christian character.

It has no saving efficacy; it is no ground of hope. The Savior warns us of the worthlessness of a hope based on miracle-working faith: "Many shall say unto me in that day, Have we not prophesied in thy name, and in thy name done many wonderful works? but then will I profess unto them, I never knew you." When the gift of faith has been bestowed, it does not necessarily bring new or deeper grace into the soul. One may be full of the grace of faith; have all the mind that was in Christ; be complete in all the will of God; be as saintly as Fletcher or Wesley, and not have the gift of faith. It does not follow because one is fully sanctified that he will have faith for healing, or other wonders. Yet not a few persons who know of the eminent piety of Dr. Steele or other holy people expect them while full of faith in all its gracious power to also possess the gift of faith which they may not at all have, because it has not been divinely conferred upon them. Not long since a noted man of God-anointed doubtless as a teacher of the deep things of spiritual life, and doing a wondrous work of evangelism, though a great cripple and sufferer -- as he was entering for the first time a church where he was to labor, a brother present having heard that he was a man of faith, said to another: "Why don't he throw away those canes?" That remark only evinced how little that person knew of the divine method respecting faith revealed in the Scriptures; that one may be full of faith, and yet not have the gift of faith, or might have the gift of faith for a work of evangelism and not for the healing of the body at all, as happened to be the case which he commented upon. Since therefore the gift of faith is not obligatory, constant, or essential, it is inferior to the grace of faith. But while it under-ranks the ordinary graces of the Holy Spirit, it is not to be discarded or depreciated, but coveted; for the apostle says, "Covet earnestly the best gifts," and then enjoins this order: "Follow after charity [love], and desire spiritual gifts;" as though he would say: Attain saving and gracious faith, even unto perfection in love, then desire and expect if it be the will of God that he impart unto you the gift of faith with its accompanying endowments.

III. Its origin.

Faith cannot exist in any form without evidence. The ground of saving faith is the written Word of the Lord promising salvation. As saving faith and faith in its fullness are given sufficient testimony on which to rest, so also faith as an endowment is provided a sure foundation by the illumination of the soul through the Holy Spirit, assuring it by the Word that God will do a given thing to, for, or by it. There are several conditions under which the gift of faith is bestowed.

1. When Praying.

He who is a man of prayer, lives much in the closet, takes everything to the Lord in prayer, most frequently receives the gift of faith at some times and in some degrees. Many of the marked cases of healing, providential deliverances, and unexpected conversions which have occurred, came as the culmination of much submissive supplication, the Holy Spirit at last saying: "According to your faith be it unto you."

2. When doing the Lord's work.

Those who are abundant in labors for God, who are faithfully executing divine missions, are not infrequently given a faith that is wonderful in its assurances and realizations. He who lives wholly consecrated to God will not be left long without works of faith. There will break in upon such a soul at times divine illuminations of God's purpose to use it as will beget a faith that shall achieve more than the removal of mountains.

3. When in great emergencies.

There come soul crises, providential straits, imminent perils, urgent necessities, and glorious possibilities, which make us cry out: "Who is sufficient for these things?" It is at such junctures that the gift of faith is often imparted, and what hitherto seemed impossible, presumptuous, and irrational becomes credible and easy.

4. When living in the fullness of the Spirit.

The normal method of the operation of the Holy Spirit in the distribution of his gifts is to confer them upon those who are saved and baptized with the Holy Ghost.

Doubtless, as the Church advances in spirituality, and the number of the fully saved multiply, the manifestation of the Holy Spirit in the gift of faith will become more frequent. This is not an uncommon endowment now, as some suppose. This gift has not been withdrawn from the Church. Every day is eventful in some as veritable works of faith as in the apostolic times, and these marvels of faith are to increase as the dispensation of the Spirit advances toward its high noon of millennial glory. Praise the Lord!

The gift of faith, like every other work of the Holy Spirit, has its own witness in the human consciousness. They who have never felt it can easily deny it, theorize against it, and decry it, and be very good people too. But it is a real experience; it is a white stone which no man knoweth but he that receiveth it. Let us live for God; pray without ceasing, keep our hearts fully saved, and then, if God may choose, he will work in us the endowment of faith; for,

"The gift of faith is all divine."

Chapter 10: The Prayer of Faith

James v, 15, 16: "The prayer of faith shall save the sick, and the Lord shall raise him up . . . The Effectual, fervent prayer of a righteous man availeth much." Jude 20: "Praying in the Holy Ghost."

The prayer of faith is a specific kind of prayer distinctively presented in the Scriptures, and so denominated, because it is an inevitable manifestation of the gift of faith.

The apostle James, in giving inspired instruction as to the method of procedure for the miraculous healing of the sick, says, "The prayer of faith shall save the sick," and then elucidates what constitutes such prayer by renaming it effectual, fervent prayer, and by presenting the praying of Elijah as a specimen of it. There has been in all ages of the Church, and there is now, a current belief, well supported by the warrant of Scripture and of Christian experience, in a kind of prayer styled prevailing prayer, which brings to pass results that prayer, in its ordinary offices, does not, and the vital factor in such prayer is the extraordinary faith which originates and accompanies it. The prayer of faith being a thing so peculiarly of its own kind in the realm of the spiritual experiences of faith, an extended treatment of it is essential to making intelligible the whole life of faith. Several discriminations respecting the prayer of faith are necessary.

I. The prayer of faith is a work of the Holy Ghost.

It is one of the offices of the Holy Spirit to inspire in the hearts of believers prevailing prayer. Romans, viii, 26: "We know not what we should pray for as we ought, but the Spirit itself maketh intercession for [in] us with groanings which

93

cannot be uttered." It is by the agency of the Holy Spirit alone that any soul is spiritually empowered to offer effectual, fervent prayer. There is a supplication in the spirit and a praying in the Holy Ghost, as such. Both the Authorized Version and the New Revision fail to convey the true meaning of the original in James v, 16. The Authorized Version reads: "The effectual, fervent prayer of a righteous man availeth much." The word fervent is superfluous, and the word effectual makes the sentence mere tautology, saying no more than that "an effectual prayer is effectual." Neither word is found in, nor suggested by, the original. The New Revision gives it thus: "The supplication of a righteous man availeth much," which is weaker still, and simply translates the word.... -- supplication or prayer -- without any rendering whatever of the attached participle in the original. The original reads: "The prayer.... of a righteous man, being energized.... avails much;" that is, prayer inwrought and empowered by the Holy Ghost in the soul of a righteous man avails much -- becomes prevailing. Such prayer, as one has said, "is an inner prayer framed within our prayer; a divine voice within our voice of supplication; God offering to himself the petitions we desire of him." The order in which the Holy Spirit works in the soul the prayer of faith is clearly revealed. First, he illuminates it, helping its spiritual inapprehension respecting what it ought to pray for beyond the sphere of gracious blessings. The righteous man knows that he ought to pray for wisdom, strength, comfort, etc., for these and like blessings are promised to him; but whether he ought to pray for recovery from sickness, or for deliverance from temporal ills, or for some other supernatural results, he does not know. But when he should pray for these things, the Holy Spirit begins to reveal them to him as allowable, and that it is the will of God to grant them, so that he is able to pray not as hitherto, "If it be thy will," but in the full persuasion that it is God's will; for the Spirit now maketh intercession for him according to the will of God. Then, accompanying this illumination, there springs up in the soul an insatiable desire for these things which the soul would not hitherto ardently desire, lest it might not maintain its submissiveness to God's will. But now the unequivocal assurance by the Holy Spirit that it is his will to do these things for it makes,

"It break out in strong desire."

It groans, not in agony, not in doubt, not in uncertainty, but in heart-longings. This groaning which enters into the experience of prevailing prayer is a depth of desire which transcends utterance, and which the most impassioned vocal supplication could but faintly express. Simultaneously with the movement of the Holy Ghost, which brings this illumination and mighty desire, there comes an assurance of faith, so as that the soul knows it has the petitions it desires of him; it rests implicitly, awaiting the realization of the things prayed for. Those who have found wrought in them the prayer of faith by the Holy Ghost will easily recognize its genesis as here delineated. The heart actuated by prayer as the immediate gift of the Holy Ghost is in the most exalted and empowered state possible in the body. It burns in a threefold flame of divine illumination, holy desire, and fervent anticipation. When this spirit of prayer seizes the soul, whether in the hush of the night watches, in the solitudes of the closet, or in the public walks of life, it irresistibly carries its suit.

Such a frame of prayer is not at our command. We cannot lift ourselves into it by any dint of effort or protracted reflection. It comes upon devout souls by the inspiration of the Holy Ghost. The Holy Spirit, in his office of inspiring prevailing prayer, is no doubt now, as ever, in continuous operation upon the hearts of believers. There are as mighty men of prayer among God's people today as ever heretofore, those of whom Elijah was but the prototype, yet unsuspected and unrecognized as being the Lord's special agents for the operation of his gracious and providential plans. But while there are many today who are occasionally or continuously baptized with this spirit of prayer, there is a promised prayer-Pentecost to visit the Church as prophetically discerned and proclaimed by Zechariah when there was disclosed to him, under the spirit of inspiration, the divine purpose, saying: "I will pour out upon the house of David and upon the inhabitants of Jerusalem the spirit of grace and of supplication."

When that outpouring of the Holy Spirit shall come upon Zion, as come it will, ushering in the grand Pentecostal era of supplication, then shall not a few only, but the whole Church pray in the Holy Ghost.

II. The prayer of faith invariably succeeds.

Success in prayer is more than access in prayer. Access is conscious audience with God; success is getting what you ask for. Paul had access to God when he prayed in repeated supplication for the healing of his body in the removal of the thorn in the flesh; but his prayer did not have success. The thorn was not removed; the cure was not granted; and simply because he did not offer the prayer of faith for it, and his lack of faith arose from his having no inwrought persuasion that it was the will of God that he should be healed. As access in prayer is a conscious, blessed experience, so also is success in prayer; it is a conscious, indubitable persuasion that the thing asked for is granted. When the saintly Fletcher of Madeley was lying in the last stages of consumption, and his condition was pronounced hopeless, John Wesley visited him, fell upon his knees at his bedside, and began to pray for his recovery. He had uttered only a few petitions when he sprang to his feet, and exclaimed: "He shall not die, but shall live and declare the works of the Lord." Wesley knew he had succeeded. Fletcher recovered and lived eight years to do the most effective work of his long and useful life. The prayer of faith does avail much. It brings to pass much that is not possible to prayer in its ordinary exercise. Prayer, in its usual offices, avails for all that is essential to spiritual life, growth in grace, and the ordinary blessing of Providence, but does not avail for special interventions in behalf of souls and the Church.

These results are only possible to inspirational prayer, or prayer in the Holy Ghost, which is distinctively the prayer of faith. The Tyndale prayer-test, insisted on a few years since, was unscientific and unreasonable, inasmuch as it proposed that any company of righteous persons who might choose should go into the ward of a hospital and pray for the recovery of a hopelessly sick patient, and, if immediate recovery should ensue, it would demonstrate the efficacy of prayer for results beyond the ordinary course of nature. In that proposition, however, there was not a single condition upon which the Bible teaches that God will heal the sick in answer to prayer. To have been a proposition compassing the Scriptural doctrine of prayer for supernatural results, it should have allowed that the suppliants must be a company of devout persons, consciously persuaded that it was the will of God to heal that patient, and believing that he would do it in answer to their prayers; or, in other words, it ought to have been a challenge to some person or persons who were consciously endowed with the gift of prayer for the healing of that patient. Inasmuch as it is not promised in God's Word that prayer, in its ordinary office, shall accomplish such supernatural results, but only prayer as a specific endowment of the Holy Ghost, the so-called test was no test at all.

The prayer of faith always succeeds. A most touching spectacle of prayer occurred seven years since when, for almost three months, all Christendom was on its knees before God in supplication for the recovery of President Garfield. Yet he did not recover, and many good people began to say: "What profit is it that we pray unto Him?" And the skeptics said: "Prayer is a failure, as we have always held." Was all that prayer useless? No; the spirit of it was eminently proper and Scriptural. The people did as they should have done; they, with prayer and thanksgiving, let their requests be made known unto God. They did say in their closets, at their family altars, and from their sanctuaries: "If it be thy will, let our Chief Magistrate live." All the prayer offered in that spirit was useful, but it was not successful; it did not avail for the President's recovery. And why? Because in all the prayers prayed no petitioner offered the prayer of faith. No one had the persuasion it would be done; no one apprehended that it was the will of God that it should be done. Everyone said: "If it be thy will." But faith never can build on a contingency, or an if; its ground is always a divine assurance, given either by the Word or the Holy Spirit of God. Had there come into the heart of the most ignorant, obscure freedman, who was a child of God, the assurance that it was the will of God to restore President Garfield, if he would believe, that humble soul might have, and doubtless would have, prayed the prayer of faith, and according to his supplication it would have been done unto him. For the prayer of faith never fails; it prospers in the thing whereunto it is sent.

Its answer is specific in kind in respect to the asking, while in degree most frequently it is above that which we think or ask. Elijah asked for rain; it came not in showers, however, but in torrents. Hannah asked for a son; he was given but was a mighty prophet as well. Hezekiah plead for life; it was given, not in a temporary respite from death, but in fifteen years of regal life. The simplicity of the prayer of faith, in its inception compared with its effectiveness, is marvelous.

Said a man to one noted for the results of his praying: "I suppose you struggle a great deal in prayer." "O no," he replied, "I scarcely know when I pray. When I desire anything of the Lord, I just look up to him in my soul and say, 'Thou wilt do it,' and feel that it will be done." When the soul is given the spirit of prevailing prayer there is fulfilled the promise (Isaiah lxv, 24), "And it shall come to pass [in the dispensation of the Holy Ghost] that before they call I will answer; and while they are yet speaking I will hear;" that is, the Holy Spirit shall inbreathe a spirit of prayer so quickly as that the soul shall receive the thing desired before the petition for it can be framed into words, and that while it is putting it in words God will be doing for it the thing desired.

It is no uncommon experience for a devout heart just to think of something it would have of the Lord, and while forming the purpose to ask it of the Lord, to be made conscious that it is granted, and the succeeding prayer for it to become rather praise that it shall be done. Praise the Lord, O my soul! The phenomenal manifestations of impassioned utterance, vehement gesticulation, or ecstatic emotions may attend or not the prayer of faith but are no essential part of its power. When Elijah opened the windows of heaven there was no demonstration, only a prostrate, voiceless form, and but for the apostle James's allusion to the wonderful event we should not have known that he prayed at all. The prayer of faith enters the heart by the inspiration of the Almighty, and never fails to rise as high as its source in almighty results. The prayer of faith being itself supernatural, what wonder is it that it accomplishes supernatural results.

III. The prayer of faith is possible only on certain conditions of heart.

1. He who offers it must be righteous. "The effectual, fervent prayer of a righteous man availeth much." "God heareth not sinners, but if any man be a worshiper of God, and doeth his will, him he heareth." God will not trust the gift of prevailing prayer with those who are discreditable in character or superficial in piety. The great men of prayer, from Abraham to William Taylor, have been godly, righteous men.

Indeed, a consciousness of being right with God is an indispensable qualification for successful prayer at all. Hence the apostle says: "Whatsoever we ask we receive of him, because we keep his commandments, and do those things which are pleasing in his sight."

If religious character is essential on the ordinary plane of prayer, how much more vital in the higher altitudes of supplication? It is only holy men whom God calls up into the mount alone with himself. Peter, James, and John were taken up by the Master to the heights of Tabor to learn the lesson of prevailing prayer, because spiritually eligible for it. A low state of Christian experience and a life of imperfect devotion to God disqualify us completely for becoming recipients of the gift of prayer. Not all who have been noted for piety have been called to be pre-eminent in prayer, but none have been noted for prayer who had not been pre-eminent for piety.

2. He who offers the prayer of faith must have faith in prayer. It is possible for one to be righteous and yet lack a profound faith in prayer itself. There are good men who have no adequate apprehension of the vital relation prayer has to God's plans and purposes; who are not impressed with its immense worth; who think of it as a mere exercise, useful to the individual, rather than being a principle of the divine government; a law by which God has chosen to effect certain results. Hence they are skeptical of prayer as a real power, and appreciate it only as a gracious movement of the heart toward God. Now, God never bestows, even upon a righteous man, the power of prevailing prayer, who, for any cause, is incredulous respecting the largest possibilities of prayer as being at present available. Faith in prayer is indispensable to praying in faith. The little child that is able to comprehend the simple precepts and promises of God's Word in respect to prayer may have a faith in prayer which will render it eligible to offer, as many a child has done, the prayer of faith. Indeed, these things are hidden from the wise and prudent, and are revealed unto babes. So the humble go on believing in prayer, and praying, believing, and see wonderful things, while the opinionated, skeptical, wise, good people go on praying, knowing none of these things in respect to prayer.

3. He who offers the prayer of faith must have the spirit of prayer. "The habit of prayer," says Mr. Spurgeon truly, "is good, but the spirit of prayer is better." This comprises an inclination to pray; a fondness for prayer; a continuous drawing out of the soul in prayer; so that, as one has said, "I am not fifteen minutes without supplication rising in my soul to God." It is taking everything to God in prayer, the soul spontaneously looking to God in care, duty, grief, service. One who has come into the spirit of holy communion with God will be fitted for the descent of the power of prevailing prayer upon him when God may choose to confer it upon him, as he doubtless will, at some times and in some measure. We do not believe anyone can long live in the practice and spirit of prayer without sooner or later having imparted to his soul the ability to offer prevailing prayer for results which are beyond the reach of prayer as a gracious exercise. Here is the profession of faith which all devout hearts make that have been baptized with the spirit of prayer.

"This is the confidence that we have in him, that if we ask any thing according to his will, he heareth us; and if we know that he hears us, whatsoever we ask we know we have the petitions that we desired of him."

Having such a spirit of prayer, the soul awaits in exultant expectation for God to do for it exceeding, abundantly above all it now thinks or asks. That is, that God will both enlarge its asking and its receiving as well. This spirit of prayer is the only soil in which God will plant the gift of faith whence springs the prayer of faith.

Dear reader, may you live in the spirit of grace and supplication, and so be fitted to receive of the Lord the gift of prevailing prayer!

Made in the USA
Middletown, DE
08 December 2023

44590252R00057